ARTHUR
THE KING IN THE WEST

R.W. DUNNING

ALAN SUTTON

First published in the United Kingdom in 1988 by
Alan Sutton Publishing Limited · Phoenix Mill · Far Thrupp
Stroud · Gloucestershire

Reprinted 1990

British Library Cataloguing in Publication Data

Dunning, R.W. (Robert William) *1938–*
    Arthur: King in the west.
    1. Legends. Characters: Arthur, King
    I. Title
    398.352

ISBN 0–86299–860–3

Designed by Richard Bryant and Martin Latham.
Typesetting and origination by
Alan Sutton Publishing Limited.
Printed in Great Britain by
The Camelot Press, Trowbridge, Wiltshire.

INTRODUCTION

THE story of King Arthur and the Knights of the Round Table has a fascination which is universal. It has attracted sculptors and painters, poets and writers of fiction, printers and typographers, musicians and dramatists, philosophers and scientists. Product of the Celtic world, it embraced in the Middle Ages the Romance of France and Italy and the Teutonic themes of Northern Europe. It was the inspiration of the Gothic Revival in 19th-century England, and its following is as strong today in California as it is in Western Europe.

But the story is not only popular; it is controversial. Historians take diametrically opposed views on its central figure, Arthur, for the written sources are few and difficult to interpret with certainty. Archaeologists are inclined to be tentative about the significance of the artefacts from the Dark Ages. Both depend on legends whose age is often unknown, whose importance is often uncertain, whose veracity cannot as yet be tested by traditional disciplines.

Yet because the story is so popular, it suffers from being over-simplified. 'Did Arthur really exist?' is a common question, but one that cannot and should not be answered simply. The story is both too important and too complex for that. It is important because it has provided an ideal to which generations have aspired, the ideal of chivalry which has had such a profound effect on our social code.

Henry III's Round Table at Winchester, Edward I's personal interest in Arthur, Edward III's Order of the Garter and Edward IV's magnificent rebuilding of St George's Chapel, Windsor, are all products of the story.

The story is also complex, for in its full flowering it embraces some elements which can be traced back to pagan Celtic mythology, some which lead through Joseph of Arimathea to the heart of the Christian Faith, some which derive from literary and poetic themes of courtly love. The modern blacksmith and the metallurgist both recognise the intensely practical elements in the apparently magical forging of Excalibur; yet to search for an armour-clad knight or many-towered Camelot in a Dark Age landscape is to search in vain, to be entirely misled.

But in the West of England there is a real landscape in which stands a fortress of obvious strength. Legends told about it at the end of the Middle Ages declared it to be Camelot, legends perhaps fostered by its owners, whose political traditions during the Wars of the Roses and later were at the heart of a revived and reviving nationalism. Modern archaeology has interpreted the site as having been refortified and reoccupied by a military leader of wealth and power. This is not 'proof' of Arthur, but is a clear indication of the importance of the legend, both as a tool to be manipulated for political ends and a guide for modern archaeologists. This book is the story of

how King Arthur, the Arthur of Legend, was brought to the West Country. It is the story of its manipulation.

Some elements in this story were firmly rooted in Cornwall from the beginning; the Welsh bards were in no doubt that Arthur's 'capital' at Kelliwic lay in the land where later writers placed Tintagel and Camlann. Somerset's role in the Dark Ages is obviously of considerable significance, but the 'Somerset' Arthur of the written sources was introduced with a clear political purpose in the 12th century, ironically through the agency of several writers from Wales whose 'ownership' of Arthur had for so long gone unchallenged.

This, then, is an attempt to trace how and why; a story of some mystery and much imagination, brilliant publicity and serious purpose. To see it as gross deception is to mistake the age and the men, for at its heart was the need to establish the Abbey of Glastonbury as the undisputed cradle of Christianity in England, in terms and in a language which the age could understand. Where other monasteries used saints to attract support, Glastonbury finally and successfully chose a popular hero and then allied him with the mystery of the Grail. It was a potent combination which kept the abbey at the forefront of English monasticism until the Dissolution, and keeps it still as a popular centre for pilgrims of all religions and of none.

But it is not simply Glastonbury whose sites –

Head of King Arthur from 13th century Germany

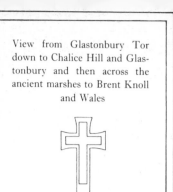

View from Glastonbury Tor down to Chalice Hill and Glastonbury and then across the ancient marshes to Brent Knoll and Wales

abbey, Tor, Wearyall Hill and Beckery – attracted visitors even in the otherwise depressing days just before the Dissolution in 1539. Its rival, Wells, may have inspired a story of Arthur on or near their land at Carhampton in West Somerset, and hence a notion that Arthur's court was near at hand, perhaps at Dunster. Brent Knoll, a Glastonbury outpost, inevitably had its tale to tell – of giants and a brave knight from Arthur's court. Further south was there not Camelot? Surely not just a notion of a friend of Sir Thomas Malory, companion in arms in the Yorkist cause. And further west are Tintagel and Camlann, the beginning and the end of the Arthurian story. The West of England is thus a treasure-house for those on the quest for the Once and Future King; and in the mysterious, misty marshes of Somerset is that sacred spot which is for many the Isle of Avalon.

THE REALM
OF THE
HERO KING

'But when did Arthur chance upon thee first?' Tennyson:
THE COMING OF ARTHUR, IDYLLS OF THE KING

SOUTH-Western Britain, the tribal lands of the Dobunni, the Durotriges and the Dumnonii, was an important part of the Roman province of Britannia, a significant fragment of the Roman Empire. Lead and silver from the Mendips and tin from Cornwall contributed to the general Imperial wealth; the healing properties of the waters of Aquae Sulis (Bath) were known far beyond Britain's shores; the corn grown and the stock reared on the larger villa estates of central Somerset were doubtless sold in distant urban markets and stored in garrison granaries. Into that same countryside, along the great Fosse Way and its offshoots, came the benefits of Rome: military protection, ordered government and the sophisticated and exotic products of Gaul and the Mediterranean.

Roman rule was, in a sense, a veneer. The native people still lived on the land accepting, some more, some less, the benefits of Empire, worshipping their native deities, some of whom acquired new names to set with the old, like Sulis Minerva at Bath; practising their traditional arts and crafts; going about their trade and commerce. The way they lived and farmed the land probably had as much to do with long-cherished social patterns as with the lie of the land and external demands.

The influence of Empire was all-pervading, the products of Empire everywhere to be seen and used. Roman coins and pottery, found even beyond the Cornish coast in the Scillies, indicate the penetra-

Above: Durotrigian coin

Opposite:
A gold Dubunnic stater

tion of Roman commerce and culture. But other Roman characteristics were alien to the far west. In the 2nd century there were only six places of significance, not necessarily even towns, in the whole country west of Bath, and none further west than the legionary fortress of Isca Dumnoniorum (Exeter). By late Roman times there were four places of importance besides Exeter, but none seems to have survived even as a village today, and their sites are not certainly known. One, Nemestatio, seems to have been in North Devon near the present Nymet place-names west of Crediton. Deventiasteno may have been somewhere in south Devon, Tamaris near the Tamar, and Durocornavis, perhaps the Rumps hillfort in North Cornwall.

Further east some of the traditional hilltop sites were abandoned. The Durotrigian strongholds of Hod Hill and Maiden Castle in Dorset were evidently attacked and destroyed by the Second Augustan Legion under Vespasian in AD 44, but two others in their territory, Cadbury and Ham Hill in Somerset, were left unharmed.

Life carried on at Cadbury almost as before, although a few people were bold enough to move outside the defences, protected by the Roman Peace, and started up a settlement at the foot of the hill which became the village of South Cadbury. Up on the hilltop business flourished: the entrance roadway was well worn, jewellery and tableware were imported from abroad, a shrine was rebuilt and

The 'Christ' roundel from the
Hinton St. Mary mosaic

visited. But two generations later there was another tale to tell, a tale of evident brutality. The Roman government probably demanded the removal of the people from their ancestral stronghold and when they tried to resist, by strengthening the rampart and barricading the south-west gate, the army took a hand. Defenders were cut down at the gate and were left where they fell; survivors were perhaps resettled in the lowlands at Catsgore or Ilchester. Cadbury's defences were destroyed, and for two centuries the site was under the plough.

In the peaceful conditions created by Rome, traders penetrated the south-west, establishing roads along the northern edge of Dartmoor and along Cornwall's spine to exploit her mineral deposits. They established river ports, in Somerset at Ilchester, Crandon and Combwich; Isca could be served as well by sea as by land. Roman technology drained the Somerset marshland around Brent Knoll and near Cheddar, and protected the low-lying pastures beside the Yeo around Yatton and Nailsea; quarried stone at Dundry and Ham Hill, mined iron ore on the Brendons; worked pewter, even made glass.

THE END OF EMPIRE

The famous letter of the Emperor Honorius of AD 410 effectually withdrawing the protection of

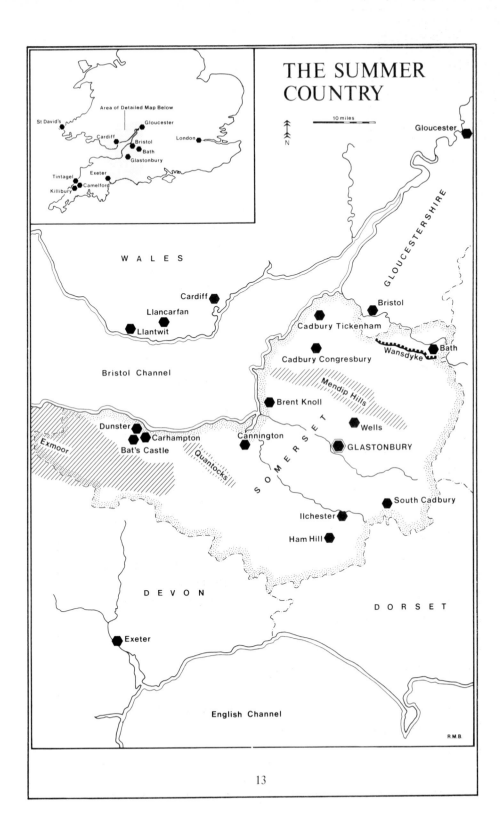

THE SUMMER COUNTRY

10 miles

N

Area of Detailed Map Below

St David's
Gloucester
Cardiff
Bristol
Bath
London
Glastonbury
Tintagel
Exeter
Killibury
Camelford

WALES

Gloucester

GLOUCESTERSHIRE

Cardiff

Bristol

Llancarfan

Cadbury Tickenham

Llantwit

Wansdyke
Bath

Cadbury Congresbury

Bristol Channel

Mendip Hills

Brent Knoll

Dunster

Wells

Exmoor

Carhampton

Cannington

SOMERSET

GLASTONBURY

Bat's Castle

Quantocks

South Cadbury

Ilchester

Ham Hill

DEVON

DORSET

Exeter

English Channel

R.M.B.

13

Magnus Maximus, proclaimed emperor by the army in Britain in 383. He withdrew vital troops from Britain for his European campaign

the Roman army from Britannia did not mark the sudden end of a civilisation. Roman army units had been withdrawn before by, for example, the usurper Magnus Maximus in 383. Rural settlements like Trethurgy in Cornwall and small towns like Ilchester were still occupied, but parts of Isca in the 4th century were already turned over to agriculture, and after AD 400 some of the walled city became a graveyard. The drainage system of the baths at Bath collapsed and the area became waterlogged. But the countryside still needed defence, and the answer in the West Country was either a return to the ancient hilltop strongholds like Chun Castle in Cornwall and South Cadbury in Somerset or, at High Peak near Sidmouth, an entirely new fortification. The rebuilt or revived fortresses and other defences like the great embankment of Wansdyke were the work of a sophisticated and efficient body of men prepared to defend a cherished way of life.

One characteristic of that way of life, eagerly sought by archaeologists, is the use of imported pottery from the eastern Mediterranean. Another, and probably more important characteristic, is Christianity. The traditions of South-Western Britain are deeply imbued with the missionary activities of a host of men and women with Welsh, Irish or Breton connections to which a later age looked back with awe. The saints of western Somerset, of North Devon and of Cornwall are not to be found by strictly archaeological means, and there is

The central motif from a 6th century North African bowl

little trace of the survival of Roman Christianity into the 5th century in the West.

Yet St Alban had been executed for his faith as long ago as AD 209 and four bishops represented the British Church at a Continental council a century later. The shrine at Henley Wood near Congresbury in Somerset may, perhaps, have been destroyed by Christians; and the latest, late 4th century, building at the old shrines on Brean Down and Lamyatt Beacon, not many miles away, may have been Christian. There is more than a suspicion, however, that Christianity was predominantly urban, at least until the remarkable visit to Britain of Victricius, Bishop of Rouen, at the invitation of some British bishops, in AD 396.

Victricius brought with him, and successfully preached, the dangerous doctrines of Ambrose and Martin; he advocated the veneration of martyrs who had suffered against unjust authority; he encouraged monastic renunciation of society; he even preached to peasants and barbarians. His success was immediate. A shrine of St Alban was established at the place of his martyrdom, a church of St Martin was built at Canterbury 'while the Romans yet inhabited Britain'; and Ninian, a disciple of Victricius, preached to the barbarians in the North and built another church in the name of St Martin at Whithorn in Galloway. Here were the beginnings of a Church on the fringes of power, a Church of the countryside.

A mounted patrol returns to the fortress at South Cadbury

A tumbled mass of stone from the destruction of the Roman temple of Sulis Minerva at Bath

The central motif from a 6th century North African bowl

About the year 540 a middle-aged man from the North – perhaps Lancashire or even Ninian's own Borderland – wrote a famous sermon. That man was called Gildas and he had been trained in his youth by a tutor who himself had a Classical education. As a man Gildas wrote for an audience of his own kind, people who could appreciate both his language and his learning and could remember what life had been like in the youthful past they all shared. Scholars are still not agreed about Gildas, though they agree about his crucial importance. Some think that he wrote in South Wales, for he was later looked upon as the founder of monastic life there. Others believe he wrote in the North-West. And where he wrote is important, for it helps to interpret what he wrote and to explain what he left unwritten.

What he wrote, a famous work called 'The Ruin of Britain', is probably the closest thing to a written history for the important century and a half after the end of official Roman rule – the Dark Ages. It was not meant to be history; it was an impassioned appeal that the civilisation and culture of his youth, and the past of which he was spiritually a part, might yet be revived by the warlords who in his time ruled the land.

Gildas saw the past as a sad decline from the civilised and ordered rule of Rome. In a 'history' written without mentioning dates, he told of invasions from the North when the Roman armies were

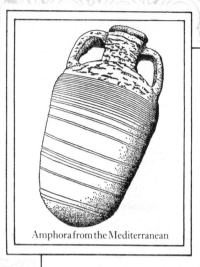
Amphora from the Mediterranean

withdrawn; of civil war and famine; then of a British revival and victory over the barbarians, followed by peace and the beginnings of kingship. After that came more barbarian invasions and an invitation to some Saxon mercenary troops to assist in their removal. The Saxons themselves revolted against their masters after initial successes; there was war, civilised city life was destroyed, and many of the British nobility retreated to Gaul. But gradually the Britons were reorganised and revived under a single leader, Ambrosius Aurelianus, who achieved a series of victories against the Saxons, culminating – and this may well have been within Gildas's own lifetime – in the Battle of Mount Badon. But, great victory that it was, it did not bring peace and the revival of culture which Gildas hoped.

Ambrosius, for Gildas, was a great warrior, 'perhaps the last of the Romans to survive', a man with an identity; no other warrior of his time was worth a name. Where, then, was Arthur, for surely Gildas, even with a northern bias, was not ignorant of the rest of Britain? Did he not denounce the petty tyrants of the West and Wales; the wicked Constantine of Dumnonia, the warlike Conan of Gloucester, the three dreadful kings of Wales? Surely he knew more of the campaigns which ended at Mount Badon than he is prepared to record? Does he name Ambrosius only to attack his descendants?

Reading Gildas alone, Gildas the near-

A Dark Age war leader

m rub o igneo. secundo modo in monte q̄
draginta dieb; & q̄draginta noctib; ieiuna
uit. tercio modo similes fuer̄ etate centū ui
ginti annis. quarto modo sepulchrū illi' ne
mo scit. S; mocculto humat̄ ꝶ nemine sci
ente. quindeci annis incaptiuitate. in uicesi
mo quinto anno. ab amatheo sco episcopo
subrogat̄. occingentorū & quinq; annorū.
inhibernia p̄dicauit. & esaut exigebat
ampli' loqui de sco patricio. sed tamen p
copendio sermonis uolui breuiare·

n illo tempore saxones inualescebant in
multitudine & crescebant inbrittannia·
Mortuo aut hengisto octha fili' ei' transi
uit de sinistrali parte brittannie ad reg
nū cantorū · & de ipso orat' reges cantoe·
une arthur pugnabat contra illos.
in illis dieb; cū regib; bricconiū· s; ipse dux erat
bellorū. Primū bellū fuit in ostiū flumi
nis quod dicit' glein. secdn. & terciū & qr
tū & quintū· sup aliud flumen quod
dicit' dubglas· q̄ in regione linnuis.
Sextū bellum sup flumen quod uoca
t̄ bassas. Septimū   fuit bellū
in silua celidonis. id; cat coit celidon·
Octauum fuit bellū in castello guinni
on. Inquo arthur portauit imagine
sce̅ marie ppetue uirginis sup humer
ros suos· & pagani uersi s̅ in fugā in
illo die. & cedes magna fuit sup illos·
p uirtutem dn̅i n̅ri ihu xp̅i & p uirtute̅
sce̅ marie uirginis genitricis ei' Nonū
bellū gestū̅ in urbe legionis. Decimū̅
gessit bellū in litore Fluminis· quod
uocat̄ tribruit· Vndecimū̅ factū̅
bellū in monte qui dicit' agned· Duo
decimū fuit bellū in monte badonis·
inquo corruer̅ in uno die ñ genti sexa
ginta uiri de uno impetu arthur·

Nennius's *Historia Britonum* describes the twelve great battles of Arthur

contemporary, Gildas the passionate preacher, that is the end of the story. But there remains ample evidence that, long before they were committed to writing, epics were sung, not just in Britain but in Ireland and Britanny, telling of another hero. Only two of these epics now survive, neither in their

A 3rd century armoured horseman from Dura Europos in the valley of the Euphrates

original form nor very near in date to their origins. One is a poem called the 'Elegy for Geraint' and the other a 'history' usually known as Nennius. The Elegy describes in vigorous language a battle (very probably at Portchester and not, as used to be thought, at Langport) where Geraint, the ruler of Dumnonia, was slain fighting in the campaign against the invaders:

'In Llongborth, I saw the clash of swords,
Men in terror, bloody heads,
Before Geraint the Great, his father's son'.

And for whom was he fighting, who was the leader who was masterminding the campaign?

'In Longborth I saw Arthur's Heroes who cut with steel;
the Emperor, ruler of our labour'.

Nennius, written in Welsh about the year 800, tells much more about this ruler, this battle leader. He describes Arthur as the man who co-ordinated the British attack in twelve battles, leading the British chieftains not simply as military supremo,

23

An early Anglo-Saxon brooch

but even perhaps as a Christian standard bearer. At the battle of Castellum Guinnion, the eighth battle, 'he carried the image of the holy Mary, the everlasting virgin, on his shield'; and in the twelfth and last, Mount Badon, 960 men fell at a single charge.

Now where do we place this 'history' in time and space? A book of annals, compiled from the late 8th century onwards at St David's and known as the Annals of Wales, mentions Arthur twice. Under the year 72 it records the battle of Mount Badon in which (but this phrase may have been added later) Arthur carried his shield with the Cross of Our Lord Jesus Christ for three days and three nights and was afterwards victorious; and under the year 93 the battle of Camlann in which Arthur and Medraut perished. That is not helpful, but at least corroborates the other references to Arthur and Badon. Modern scholars, concerned to make the matter fit into the context of conventional history, date Badon between 480 and 520 and, with less confidence, place it somewhere in southern England, mentioning as possible sites Solsbury Hill near Bath, the earthworks at Badbury Rings in Dorset, or Liddington Castle near Badbury in Wiltshire.

Yet there are still some doubts. Some doubt the very existence of an individual Arthur, preferring some personification of Celtic opposition. Some see him as a figure from another time, when the struggle against the barbarian was in its infancy long before

ci sunt usq; ad decu & ualenanu. anni
sunt sexaginta noue.

an	an · ccc ·	an
an	an	an
an	an	an
an	an	dn
an	an	an
an,	an	an · lxx ·
an	an	an
an,	an	an Bellu badonis inq
an, Pasca co	an	arthur portauit cruce
mutatur sup dñi	an · xl ·	dñi nri ihu xpi · trib;
em diei cum	an	dieb; & trib; noctib;
papa leone epi	an	inhumeros suos &
rome.	an	brittones uictores fuer.
an · x · Brigida	an	an,
sci nascitur.	an	an,
an	an	· an,
an	an	an,
an Scs Patrici	an	an Scs colu cille nasc.
ad dñm migra	an	Qui esse brigide.
tur.	an · l ·	an,
an	an	an,
an,	an,	an · lxxx ·
an	an	an,
an,	an,	an,
an,	an,	an,
an	an	an,
an · xx ·	an Epis ebur pau an,	
an	cu mxpo an	an,
an	no · cael · etatis	an,
an	sug ·	· an,
an quies benigni	an	an,
epi.	an	an · xc ·
an,	an · lx ·	an,
an,	an,	an,
an,	an,	an Gueith camlan inq
an	an	arthur & medraut
an	an	corruer. & mortalitas

The Welsh Annals record the battles of Mount Badon and Camlann

Gildas's time. Some even suggest a later period when the struggle continued on the fringes of the Saxon kingdoms. And there is, and can be, no absolute proof.

TRADITION AND ARCHAEOLOGY

Tradition and the evidence of archaeology between them plead strongly for what cannot be proved, an Arthur of the West Country and Wales, an Arthur who co-ordinated the power of hillfort chieftains, an Arthur who led fast-moving cavalry to military success, an Arthur who could have known Glastonbury. Tradition takes us to the mysterious 'king-lists', royal genealogies which play such an important part in Welsh historical studies. One of these was compiled in South-East Wales to demonstrate the long royal descent of Morgan ap Owain, King of Morgannwg, another traced a line of princely saints. And in both, far back at a time when the memory of man ran not to the contrary, was the royal line of the kings of Dumnonia: Constantine of Cornwall, father of Erbin, father of Geraint, father of Cadwy. Was this the Constantine denounced by Gildas? Was this the Geraint who brought his men east to fight for Arthur against the barbarian and lost his life? Was this the Cadwy who ruled with Arthur at Dindraithou?

King-lists and the many other Welsh literary sources, some of them known to Geoffrey of Monmouth and some still surviving, are not strictly

history. By the time they were written down they had long been part of an oral tradition, and their Dumnonian origins can only be dimly discerned within the Welsh tradition. By the 9th century Constantine, Geraint and Cadwy had become Welsh folk heroes. So is there nothing left of Dumnonia, nothing more solid than sagas and vague stories? Is there no trace of a hero in the Land of Summer, no chieftain fighting from his hilltop stronghold?

If there are historical doubts about the heroes of Dumnonia, there is no doubt about a stone monument that stands near Castle Dore in southern Cornwall. The stone bears in Latin the words 'Here lies Drustan, son of Cunomorus' which, being interpreted is 'Here lies Tristan, son of Cynfawr'; and Cynfawr (who might also be Mark) is in the king-list of Dumnonia, the father of Constantine of Cornwall. And real enough, on Cornwall's north coast, was the monastery on the headland once called by the Irish Rosnant and now Tintagel. This was a school for saints in the Irish tradition, a centre of both religion and culture. And there have been found those fragments of pottery which are in many ways the key to the Dark Ages in the West. Those fragments are the remains of vessels for wine, oil, and perhaps even fruit from the far Mediterranean, the wine and oil bespeaking ritual use as well as sophisticated palates. Heroes and saints there were indeed in Dumnonia.

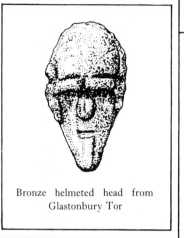

Bronze helmeted head from Glastonbury Tor

But Cornwall was, for many years to come, far from the front line in the struggle for survival. The real challenge was further east and there, in the Land of Summer, Somerset, sophistication and Christian culture seem to go hand in hand with organised and powerful regional government, and a military force able to stand up successfully to the Saxon threat.

Archaeologists have found the same Mediterranean pottery and high quality metalwork at Cadbury–Congresbury, on Glastonbury Tor, and on the great hillfort of South Cadbury. It is likely that other Iron-Age strongholds were re-occupied like them – notably Brent Knoll, Cadbury–Tickenham and Bat's Castle, the last one of a triumvirate of forts around the later site of Dunster Castle. Two more such hillforts, Maes Knoll and Stantonbury, are integral parts of the massive linear earthwork called Wansdyke which may well have marked the frontier of a British Kingdom against the Saxon enemy. And such a vast undertaking as Wansdyke involved considerable administrative organisation as well as military expertise. Another hillfort, at Cannington, is associated not only with some sort of permanent settlement, but with a cemetery, part pagan and part Christian, in which some graves were placed as if in deference to a single tomb, the tomb of a youth. Was he, like the nephew of Caratacus named on the stone of Winsford Hill, the offspring of a noble Christian house, a ruler, the

The Caratacus Stone, Winsford Hill, Somerset

Wansdyke snakes its way across Wiltshire and North Somerset, a frontier boundary of a British Kingdom

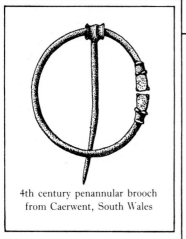

4th century penannular brooch
from Caerwent, South Wales

like of whom may have occupied the hilltop strongholds further east?

Perhaps supreme above all these leaders was he who ruled from the height of South Cadbury, he whose men crowded into the great timber hall on its summit. Cadbury is on a scale requiring vast resources, constructed for an army large by the standards of the time. It occupies a site of strategic importance, a base for action deep into Saxon-held territory, in a country within striking distance of the acceptable sites for the great victory of Mount Badon. Could Cadbury have been the springboard for the final triumph of the leader of battles?

GEOFFREY OF MONMOUTH AND THE GROWTH OF ROMANCE

The earliest written sources which refer to Arthur are themselves evidence of his continuing and increasing popularity. Nennius and the Annals of Wales were part of a growing body of writing, of which nothing else now survives, which by the late 8th century had made Arthur a Welsh hero. He became, naturally enough, a popular figure in Welsh literature; his name is found in the Welsh Triads, the titles which served as aides memoires which the bards used to remember the stories they told. Arthur's followers by the end of the 11th century people the stories known collectively as the Mabinogion, stories part mythological, part drawn from the French Romances.

Arthur appears, too, by the late 11th century in those peculiar literary devices known as Lives of Saints. Four survive, all probably written by Welshmen in praise of Welshmen, two from the monastery of Llan-

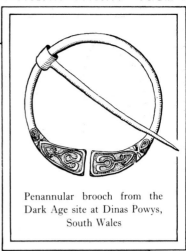

Penannular brooch from the Dark Age site at Dinas Powys, South Wales

carfan. They tell of the holy behaviour and remarkable deeds of Cadoc and Padarn, Carantoc and Gildas. The saint is, of course, the hero of each, but one character is common to all, Arthur. In all four Lives, he is something of a rogue and petty tyrant, converted to higher deeds and attitudes by the influence of the saint in question. St Cadoc found him as a quarrelsome ruler of easy morals, dicing on a hilltop with his companions Kay and Bedivere; St Padarn met him as a man who laid covetous eyes on the saint's tunic. St Carantoc encountered him as a ruler unable to subdue a dragon which was devastating his realm and as a petty thief who tried to convert the saint's portable altar into a domestic table. St Gildas found him as a ruler who could brook no opposition but a husband whose wife had been taken to Glastonbury by Melwas, King of the Summer Country.

It is clear that the stories of Arthur were known and established by the early 12th century throughout the Celtic world and beyond. Some canons of Laon, visiting the West Country in 1113, were shown Arthur's Chair and Arthur's Oven, probably on Dartmoor in Devon, and in Cornwall

Arthur defeats King Lucius

they nearly provoked a riot at Bodmin by refusing to believe a local who asserted that Arthur was not dead. William of Malmesbury, the 'official' historian of Glastonbury Abbey, knew an Arthur of history and an Arthur, as he devastatingly described him, of 'lying fables'; he accepted the evidence of Nennius as accurate, but he was less than happy with the literary embroidery which seemed by his time to have overtaken it.

And that literary embroidery reached its full flowering in the work of Geoffrey of Monmouth, who between about 1130 and 1136 or 1138 wrote his greatest work, the 'History of the Kings of Britain'. Geoffrey, Cornishman, Breton or Welshman, was a cleric rather by accident; by choice he was a scholar and a romantic, and the learning of Oxford for once found popular expression in his literary genius. But was it all embroidery? William of Newburgh, writing about 1190, declared: 'It is quite clear that everything this man wrote about Arthur and his successors . . . was made up, partly by himself, or for the sake of pleasing the Britons'. That is one opinion. Geoffrey himself claimed that he based part of his book 'The Prophesies of Merlin' on stories he had heard from his friend Alexander, Bishop of Lincoln; and he stated more than once that his source for his History was 'a certain very ancient book written in the British language' given to him by another friend, Walter, Archdeacon of Oxford.

Arthur defeats King Lucius

Scholars argue a good deal about Geoffrey's sources, but there is general agreement that his work owes something to his own scholastic background (he knew the works of Gildas, Bede and Nennius); something to the traditions of the Celtic world to which he belonged; and very much to his own fertile imagination and literary bent. And it owes something, too, to his own desire for advancement. Geoffrey dedicated his History jointly to Robert, Earl of Gloucester, illegitimate son of Henry I, and to Waleran, Count of Mellent, son of Robert de Beaumont. They were powerful men.

Geoffrey's work was a literary success, a best seller in medieval terms; more than two hundred copies still survive. William of Newburgh was one of the few who considered it unreliable at the time. For almost six centuries afterwards it was accepted as actual history; but more than that, it created the Arthur most people still recognise: a larger-than-life figure possessed of a wonderful sword, protected by the magic of Merlin, ruling over a splendid court, conquering an empire beyond the sea. There was just enough history in Geoffrey's work to make it acceptable; and just enough reality to make it entirely plausible. Part of that reality was to give Arthur a topographical base. He was no longer vaguely Welsh, as the older sources had implied; he was South-Western and particularly Cornish. He was the successor to a kingdom sometimes almost independent, successor to a Cornish dynasty which

Camlann

had once ruled the whole of Britain. First and last, Arthur was Cornish; he was conceived at Tintagel, and his final battle, Camlann, was fought by the river Camel. Perhaps Geoffrey's own origins suggested Caerleon on Usk as the site of Arthur's court, but that was almost an aberration.

Tintagel was the significant choice. Its importance in the history of the Celtic South-West may well still have been remembered in the 12th century; and its owner in Geoffrey's day was none other than Reginald, another illegitimate son of Henry I, half-brother to Robert, Earl of Gloucester, who was married to a Cornish heiress and was soon to hold the Cornish earldom. And here about 1141 – could it have been inspired by Geoffrey himself? – Reginald built a castle.

Geoffrey has been credited with political flattery, implying that the Norman kings were the true successors of the great kings of the British past, and that the Norman nobility were the modern mirrors of their faithful followers. Was it, therefore, a continuation of that flattery to suggest that Arthur had been saved from a mortal death? Might he not still live on in the good deeds of the House which now ruled the land? But if so, where did he rest? Geoffrey was not at all specific; Arthur went to Avalon for the healing of his wounds. Of course Geoffrey knew of Glastonbury; it was not Glastonbury.

THE CLAIMS
OF THE
PAST

'. . . but it lies deep-meadow'd, happy, fair with orchard-lawns
and bowery hollows crown'd with summer sea. . .'
Tennyson: MORTE D' ARTHUR

Ring-knot from an Anglo-Saxon
stone cross at Glastonbury

AT the time of the Norman conquest, the Abbey at Glastonbury was the richest monastery in the land. As the Saxon kings had established their rule down the western peninsula the abbey had been favoured so that its lands stretched far from its home in the central lowlands of Somerset. King Cynewulf had given land at Culmstock in Devon about 670 and his successor, Ine, after his victory over Geraint of Cornwall, had given an estate further west, between the Tamar and the Lynher. Another large estate, in the Torridge Valley of Devon, was the next addition, about 729, and King Egbert, in about 855, gave more land in north Devon, the old minster at Braunton. By the time of Domesday, however, these lands had slipped from Glastonbury's grasp: Braunton had passed to the Crown, Culmstock to the bishop of Exeter. The abbey's sole estate in Devon by 1086 was Uplyme; in Cornwall it possessed nothing at all.

GLASTONBURY UNDER PRESSURE

The abbey remained vulnerable to the jealous eyes of its new neighbours, the men from across the Channel who came with the Conqueror to supplant the Anglo-Saxon landowners, once the abbey's good friends and benefactors. Abbots Aethelweard and Aethelnoth, if later historians are to be believed, had led their house into decline even before the Con-

queror came, and it was
unable to withstand the
demands of the new land-
lords. Aethelweard was
remembered by the abbey's
historians because he
exhumed the remains of
King Edgar and crammed
them into a casket with the
relics of St Vincent and St
Apollinaris. Aethelnoth sold

Ring-knot from an Anglo-Saxon
stone cross at Glastonbury

some of the abbey's treasures, including gold and
silver ornaments which had been given by Bishop
Brihtwold of Ramsbury fifty years earlier.

The reward of these profligates was fitting.
Aethelweard went out of his mind and not long
afterwards broke his neck as he left the abbey
church. Aethelnoth, who gave the abbey estate at
Batcombe to his own mother, much to the
annoyance of the monks, withdrew to Normandy
with the Conqueror and stayed there until 1077–8,
when he was deposed and retired to Canterbury
Cathedral Priory. For Glastonbury monks that fate
might well have been accounted madness.

Beyond these ancient memories of decline from
the high standards of St Dunstan's time, there is the
factual record of Domesday Book. In 1066, while
Edward the Confessor was still alive, Glastonbury's
estate in Somerset alone amounted to over 473 hides
of land. Twenty years later the abbey had lost over
67 hides, mostly to the Bishop of Coutances and the
Count of Mortain, a loss greater than the whole
estate of the neighbouring monastery of Muchelney.
The historian William of Malmesbury, writing fifty
years later, was still conscious of the grudge felt by

Anglo-Saxon ring-knot

the community at such treatment: the house, he declared, had been 'almost stripped' of its estates by the 'hostile assaults and violent oppression', first of the Danes and then of the Normans. That was a fair reflection of Glastonbury feeling; to Saxon monks, Norman and Dane were much the same.

The removal of Aethelnoth did not end the trouble. In his place the king and Archbishop Lanfranc appointed Thurstan, a monk of Caen. At first he proved himself a worthy successor to Dunstan, establishing not only the abbey's supremacy over the little Benedictine houses of Muchelney and Athelney but also its independence of the bishops of the diocese. At a meeting before Lanfranc, sometimes called the Council of the Parrett, Thurstan argued 'with great and steady eloquence' on behalf of his house, quoting royal charters from Centwine and Ine to prove Glastonbury's liberties against the counter claims of the Bishop of Wells. It was a great victory; Wells, so Thurstan's supporters claimed, 'departed without glory or honour'.

But it was for Thurstan a temporary victory. Soon afterwards he was involved in a dreadful incident which profoundly shocked contemporary opinion. Behaving more like an autocrat than a caring pastor, he first proposed a more strict rule of life than the monks had been used to, and then demanded the introduction of a foreign chant for the liturgy. Glastonbury monks were nothing if not traditiona-

Glastonbury Tor, from the South-West

The Somerset Levels in flood.
When the waters receded the
land appeared as the Summer
Country.

The Magna Tabula, the late-14th century Glastonbury guide book

St. Dunstan kneels at the feet of Christ: a page from 'St. Dunstan's Classbook'.

lists, and finally their opposition drove Thurstan to action. He called in a group of soldiers to compel obedience. Norman knights fought Saxon monks as the religious retreated into their church and barricaded themselves in the choir. Hiding behind benches and armed only with candlesticks, they were no match for arrows fired from a gallery above. Two, and perhaps three, monks were killed and a dozen or so wounded.

When the king heard of the incident, Thurstan was quickly taken back to Normandy; many of the monks, too, were moved away and kept under guard in other monasteries. Norman could not condone such opposition, even against brutal Norman. Glastonbury, almost in defiance, retained a relic of that dreadful time. During the fighting an arrow pierced a crucifix held by one of the monks and the figure of Christ was damaged below the knee. A miraculous stream of blood from the wound actually brought the attack to an end, and the soldier who fired the arrow immediately went mad. The crucifix was thereafter venerated, and still in the 14th century, according to John of Glastonbury, the trace of the wound was clearly visible.

Most of Glastonbury's losses to the new Norman landowners must have occurred when Thurstan was abbot (c 1077/8–1096–+). His successor, Abbot Herluin (1100–18), another Caen monk, was remembered as a great builder and benefactor, and some of the lost land was recovered. The next abbot,

The West Front, Wells Cathedral, consecrated 1239

Seffrid Pelochin (1120/1–1125), a monk of Seez and brother of Archbishop Ralph of Canterbury, gave away at least three manors to a relative, thus undoing much of the work of his predecessor. The task facing the next abbot was considerable.

But the man was equal to the task. A young monk from Cluny, under thirty years of age, able and well connected, Henry of Blois was a nephew of King Henry I and brother of Henry's successor, King Stephen. A man of undoubted financial and administrative flair and wide cultural sympathies, Henry was appointed Abbot of Glastonbury in 1126, and three years later also became Bishop of Winchester. He held both offices until his death in 1171.

As soon as he arrived at Glastonbury, Henry set about the restoration of the abbey's finances and the creation of a splendid group of monastic buildings. Recent excavations at the abbey exposed the massive wall footings of Abbot Henry's 'palace', south-west of the present Lady Chapel, and finely carved stonework in the Abbey Museum is witness to the high quality of the work in the cloister, chapter house, refectory, dormitory and infirmary.

But in order to pay for this work the lost estates had to be recovered, and even with Abbot Henry's power and influence the task was not easy. The Glastonbury chroniclers record that he won back the manors of Mells, Uffculme, Camerton and Damerham, several villages along the Polden ridge, the island of Nyland, and pieces of land in Brent Marsh.

Wells Cathedral

To make sure that these and its other estates were protected for the future, the abbot secured the approval of three popes, who issued formal charters confirming ownership to the abbey: Pope Innocent II in 1137, Pope Lucius II in 1144, and Pope Alexander III in 1168. In the eyes of the Church Universal, Glastonbury's lands were secure.

Yet still there were threats to the abbey's independence. Bishop Giso of Wells had tried unsuccessfully in Abbot Thurstan's time to question Glastonbury's privileges, and his successors would doubtless try again. From another direction, the monks had recently been challenged most rudely by Osbern of Canterbury, who, in his Life of St Dunstan, had dismissed Glastonbury's claim to be an ancient foundation by suggesting that the saint had been its first abbot! Eadmer, another Canterbury monk, had gone further by contradicting the Somerset claim that Dunstan's bones had been rescued from Canterbury to save them during Viking raids.

THE ATTRACTIONS OF SANCTITY

So in face of these pressures the monks of Glastonbury, English to their fingertips, determined to re-establish their traditions. They were themselves in no doubt that the history of their house reached back beyond the time of written record. Each

generation of monks had passed to the next the belief that the wattle church at the heart of their monastery was, of a truth, the earliest Christian shrine in the land. But there was nothing to prove it. Now this belief must be established beyond doubt. The saints of Glastonbury must be recorded, both to raise the spirits of a depressed community and to encourage recruitment. And, perhaps, more generally, to raise the level of public interest in a house which needed the support of patrons and pilgrims.

The monks turned, therefore, to two men to lead them out of their difficulties. They were men of very different talents, the one a hagiographer, that is a writer of saints' lives, the other an historian. Caradoc of Llancarfan, the hagiographer, who had already written a Life of Cyngar for the canons of Wells as well as Lives of St Cadoc and probably St Illtud for his own house of Llancarfan in Wales, compiled for Glastonbury a Life of St Gildas. Hagiographers by their very calling had a special purpose, namely to tell the story of their subject not in strictly historical terms, but rather with the object of creating a sense of devotion. Caradoc, like many of his kind, wove the few known facts about Gildas with tales from other sources about other saints and the products of his own imagination into a narrative quite unacceptable as history.

There is, for example, no doubt that Gildas was venerated at Glastonbury in the 11th century; and it is at least possible that he spent some time there. But

The chapel of St. Gildas near Carhaix – Plouguer, Britanny

it is quite clearly nonsense for Caradoc to claim that Gildas died at Glastonbury and was buried there before the altar. The traditions of the saint in Britanny are not only earlier but essentially more likely. The saint lies buried behind the high altar of the church of St Gildas-de-Rhuis in Morbihan. But, historically accurate or not, one element in Caradoc's Life of Gildas above all others is of the greatest interest. It appears to be the first time that Glastonbury and Arthur were linked together in writing.

This story may well have been told at Glastonbury before Caradoc gave it some respectability, and there is no doubt that he used it to advantage in his tale. He recounted how Gildas, coming to the abbey, found that Melwas, King of the Summer Country, was in conflict with King Arthur, having abducted Guinevere and held her at his stronghold. Gildas, as might be expected, mediated between the rivals, Guinevere was returned to her lord, and the two chieftains, promising always to follow Gildas's counsel, gave much territory to the Church.

A year or two before Caradoc came to Glastonbury the monks invited William of Malmesbury to perform a similar service. He came to the abbey about 1129, commissioned to write Lives of four Glastonbury saints, Patrick, Benignus, Indracht and Dunstan. Now William was an historian and something of an archaeologist rather than a hagiographer, and his Lives were not exactly what the monks expected. William found, for instance, no proof that Glaston-

William of Malmesbury's 'History of Glastonbury'

bury had ever recovered the bones of Dunstan from Canterbury, and he could not bring himself to pretend otherwise. He felt much the same about other tales the monks told him; but reluctant to reject anything so dear to his hosts, he carefully distinguished what he believed from what he did not.

So the results were a disappointment to the monks. In his preface to his more famous history of Glastonbury, William explained how he had submitted his Lives to the community 'so that if anything unreasonable had been said it could be properly corrected'. The monks deliberated at length and finally assessed the works favourably, agreeing that 'nothing in them gave offence to religious eyes or lacked graciousness'. But their judgement clearly lacked enthusiasm.

So William embarked on a much more important task, nothing but the complete story of Glastonbury from its foundation. He was, of course, faced again with the problem of fact versus legend; and again he made it clear that he believed some of the monks' traditions and not others. But he endeavoured to tell the story in all its richness from the very beginnings: the story of twelve disciples sent by the Apostle Philip, the story that the first Christian converts found at Glastonbury an ancient church 'prepared by God himself for human salvation . . . consecrated to himself and to Mary, the Holy Mother of God'. History or not, it was a bold claim.

FIRE

AND

VAPOUR OF SMOKE

'And truth is this to me, and that to thee; and truth or clothed or naked let it be' . . .' Tennyson: THE COMING OF ARTHUR, IDYLLS OF THE KING

HISTORY, however, was evidently not enough; that must be the inference. For within a very few years of the appearance of William of Malmesbury's 'De Antiquitate Glastoniensis Ecclesia', his history of the Church of Glastonbury, other hands had added what William himself had not chosen to include, others claimed as history what William had barely recognised as respectable legend. And the reasons for such alterations were the same as those which had prompted the monks to invite him and Caradoc a generation earlier. Glastonbury was under pressure again.

In the 12th century there was a great extension of monasticism as the new Orders – the Cluniacs, the Cistercians and the Augustinians – established themselves. They were, consciously or unconsciously, the rivals of the long-established Benedictines, competing for both patronage and recruits. In Somerset, Glastonbury thus found itself with popular new monastic neighbours, some like Montacute or Witham offering a stricter and more simple Rule, others such as Taunton, Bruton and Keynsham a more relaxed discipline.

And the claims of the bishops of Bath became more pressing. The end of the rule of Abbot Henry of Blois in 1171 was followed first by a vacancy of well over a year, and then by the election of Robert, until then Prior of Winchester. John of Glastonbury, the abbey's historian writing in the 14th century, recorded that Robert was 'adorned with the

flower of all virtues and a special lover of the poor' but he had to admit that 'with rather less wisdom' the abbot had been outwitted by Bishop Reginald of Bath. Robert had been induced to become a member of the Chapter of Wells, and thus the bishop's subordinate. And, in establishing that his control of the central churches on the abbey's estate was secure, the abbot was obliged by the bishop to give up the church of South Brent as compensation to the Archdeacon of Wells. The first arrangement was soon repudiated, but the churches of Pilton and Ditcheat were permanently lost to Wells.

There was a nine-year vacancy following Abbot Robert's death in 1180, nine years of crisis and tragedy. For four years from 1189 Glastonbury was ruled by Henry de Sully, formerly prior of the Cluniac house at Bermondsey. Abbot Henry's great success was to obtain from Pope Celestine III in 1191 the right for himself and his successors to wear the mitre, ring and other trappings of a bishop. John of Glastonbury, writing in the 1340s but incorporating contemporary material, marvelled how a man like Abbot Henry could make such efforts on behalf of his house, but at the same time could contemplate leaving his flock to the teeth of a wolf. That wolf was Savaric FitzGeldewin, Bishop of Bath, who engineered the removal of Abbot Henry to the bishopric of Worcester and contrived his own appointment as Abbot of Glastonbury in 1193. For the next seven years or so the monks made concerted efforts to rid

The North Doorway of the Lady Chapel, Glastonbury Abbey

themselves of their unwanted abbot-bishop. There was violence, and for a short time the house lay under an interdict; the monks were divided among themselves and their spiritual state was at a very low ebb. Yet the community survived not only these troubles, but a still greater tragedy.

The Lady Chapel, Glastonbury

DISASTER AT GLASTONBURY

On the feast of St Urban (25 May) 1184 a devastating fire destroyed the monastic buildings at Glastonbury, leaving only a chamber and chapel built by Abbot Robert and the bell-tower built by Abbot Henry of Blois. Gold, silver, silks, books, ornaments and other furnishings were reduced to ashes and formless lumps of metal; the holy relics of the past were either charred or hopelessly confused. There was no abbot to take a lead; moans, tears and lamentations were to be heard on all sides.

Soon after the fire the king, who had hitherto been enjoying the income of the abbey in the absence of an abbot, appointed his chamberlain, Ralph FitzStephen, to take charge of the work of rebuilding. And so efficiently did Ralph carry out his task that, apparently within a year or two, the Lady Chapel, built on the site of the old church, was finished in the 'most attractive workmanship' which can still be enjoyed today. Ralph also began the restoration of the conventual buildings – presum-

ably some of the walls had been left standing – and, using the stone from Abbot Henry's 'palace' and the precinct wall, laid out the massive foundations of a new abbey church.

But there was more to recovery than renewing buildings. The abbey's precious relics had to be put in order and more widely publicised if Glastonbury was to keep pace with the rival attractions of Abingdon and Ely, Westminster and especially Canterbury. The first stage was to exhume the bodies of St Patrick, St Indracht and St Gildas from near the altar in the Old Church and place them in suitable shrines. The second stage was the remarkably fortunate discovery of an ironbound wooden chest containing the bones of St Dunstan, complete with his episcopal ring on one finger. The painted initials S and D at each end of the chest left no-one in any doubt of their authenticity, whatever Canterbury might claim. A special gold and silver shrine was made to contain the bones in proper state, a shrine which was later to be shared with the shoulder and forearm of St Oswald.

Building work, of course, continued and 'a large part' of the abbey church was finished when Henry II died. Work then seems to have come to a halt until the appointment of Henry de Sully as abbot; and he, it seems, had little enthusiasm for building. The monks, therefore, had to take matters into their own hands, carrying relics and indulgences around the country to raise funds. Their success, on their

own admission, was only moderate. Something more effective had to be done. It is not certain where the idea of King Arthur at Glastonbury first came from. There may well have been folk tales relating to the place in Celtic mythology, for the topography of the area and its often mysterious weather pattern must have given rise in a more impressionable age to many flights of fancy.

THE DISCOVERY OF ARTHUR

Caradoc of Llanfarcan is the first, apparently, to claim an historical connexion as early as the 1130s when he brought Arthur to the place in search of Guinevere. But William of Malmesbury in his comprehensive history did not mention Arthur, and for sixty years the monks looked to other methods to support their cause. Yet the relics of St Gildas, St David, St Patrick and the rest proved neither convincing nor popular. The discovery of the relics of King Arthur was a masterstroke.

Apparently, no doubts were raised about the discovery until the 20th century but there is no surviving eye-witness account of such an important event, and the near-contemporary sources do not agree on many points. Therein, if for no other reason, lies the suspicion.

Evidently the earliest version of the story comes from Wales, from a chronicler at the abbey of Margam who may well have had before him Glaston-

Glastonbury Abbey:
the crossing, looking east

bury's official report in the form of a circulated newsletter. The Margam chronicler describes how one of the monks had 'begged and prayed' to be allowed to be buried in the ancient cemetery, at a spot between the two ancient cross shafts which bore a series of names in almost indecipherable writing. So when the monk died, about 1191, a grave was dug in the place he had chosen. First the diggers came upon a coffin containing the bones of a woman, with the hair still intact. Beneath it they found a second coffin containing the bones of a man; and below that they found a third, on which a leaden cross was fixed which was inscribed with the words in Latin 'Here lies the famous King Arthur buried in the isle of Avalon'. Inside this third coffin were the bones of a large man. The first tomb, declared the chronicler, was that of 'Guinevere, wife of the same Arthur; the second, that of Mordred, his nephew; the third that of the aforesaid prince'.

The second record of the discovery is by another Welshman (why were the Welsh so keen to give Somerset the credit?), the popular writer and publicist Gerald of Wales – a sensible choice if the monks wished to broadcast their success. Gerald visited Glastonbury within a fairly short time of the discovery and described both the leaden cross, which he actually handled, and a thigh bone and a skull, both of remarkable size, which Abbot Henry de Sully showed him. But by the time of his visit the story had significantly changed.

Glastonbury Abbey:
the crossing, looking east

Gerald prefaced his description with a swipe at 'popular stories' about Arthur which had the 'fantastic' ending that the king was 'carried away to a remote place and was not subject to death'. Of course there was a body. Gerald declared that records of the abbey contained 'signs' of the body's presence in Glastonbury, and the letters inscribed on the cross shafts in the cemetery, although 'almost obliterated by age' suggested the same. Further, 'visions and revelations' had been seen by 'holy men and clerks'; and, finally, King Henry II himself had been told by a Welsh bard (the Welsh again) that Arthur's body would be found sixteen feet down in the earth in a hollow oak, all rather different from the accidental discovery recorded by the Margam chronicler.

What was found had changed, too. The actual discovery was accompanied by 'wonderful and miraculous signs', perhaps necessary to encourage the diggers. Deep down, so Gerald declared, there was first a stone, under which the leaden cross was fixed. And then the coffin, only one, but divided; two thirds at the head contained the bones of a man, one third at the foot the bones of a woman, together with a tress of golden hair which turned to dust when touched by an eager monk. There was no third coffin, no third body. And the words on the cross were not as the Margam chronicler reported: 'Here lies buried the famous King Arthur with Guinevere his fortunate wife in the isle of Avalon'.

A third chronicler, Ralph of Coggeshall, writing about 1193, mentioned the discovery briefly. For him, as for the Margam chronicler, it was accidental, the result of the wish of the dying monk. And the words on the leaden cross made no mention of Guinevere. The two later Glastonbury chroniclers, Adam of Domerham and John of Glastonbury, added their own details, declaring that there were two tombs, and that during the excavations curtains had been placed around the site.

Doubts have reasonably been raised, even on the evidence of these sources. Two facts are not open to question. One is that a hole was dug between the two cross shafts in the monks' cemetery; traces of that excavation were clearly seen during the excavations in the 1960s. The other is that the cross was real. John Leland in Henry VIII's time held it in his hands. It measured, he wrote, nearly a foot in length, and the words it bore were those reported by the Margam chronicler. The antiquary William Camden published a drawing of it in 1607, the only clue to its characters, and it has been lost to sight since the 18th century. It cannot thus be submitted to scientific study which might prove it a 12th century forgery or a genuine product of the 6th century. But genuine or not does not now matter. The cross 'proved' Glastonbury to be Avalon and the bones to be Arthur's. That was enough.

But just in case the bones were not entirely convincing, the Margam chronicler, presumably

William Camden's drawing of the Arthur Cross (1607)

briefed by the Glastonbury monks, indulged in a little etymology. Glastonbury must be the Isle of Avalon for it used to be an island surrounded by marshes, and 'aval' in the British language meant apple. Gerald of Wales went further into the matter: one of the old names for Glastonbury was Inis Avallon, the applebearing island; another name was Inis Gutrin (otherwise Yniswithrin), the Isle of Glass, hence the Saxon name Glastingeburi, 'for in their tongue glas means glass and a camp or town is called buri'. Modern place-name experts would not accept such a specious explanation.

THE TOMB OF THE KING

Once found, the bones of Arthur and Guinevere were translated into the (presumably still unfinished) abbey church and placed in a tomb in the centre of the choir, at the heart of the liturgical life of the community. Not much less than a century later the tomb was opened, the high point in an event stage-managed to perfection by the able Abbot John of Taunton.

John of Glastonbury tells in detail how in 1278 the young Edward I and Queen Eleanor, accompanied by Archbishop Kilwardby of Canterbury, came to spend Easter at the abbey. Three times during those few days the abbot pointedly maintained the privileges of his house in the Liberty

The site of King Arthur's Tomb, Glastonbury Abbey

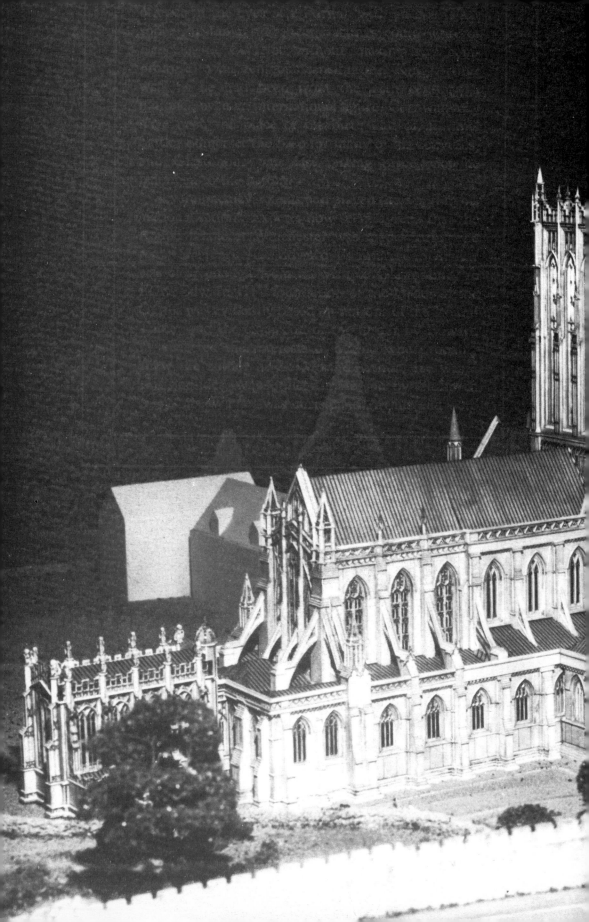

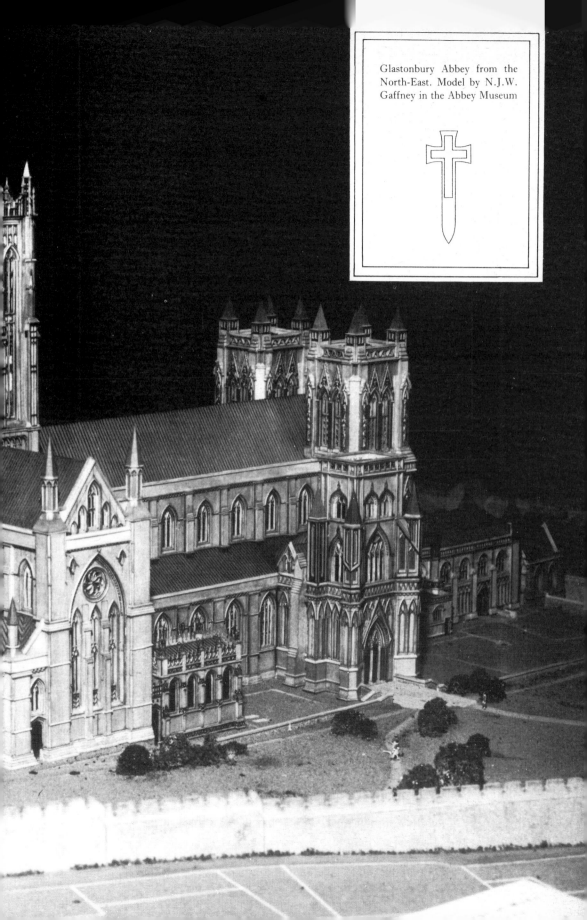

Glastonbury Abbey from the North-East. Model by N.J.W. Gaffney in the Abbey Museum

of the Twelve Hides, first by refusing the Earl Marshal's claims to take lodgings for the royal retinue; second by taking an offender against the king into his own custody; and third by successfully resisting the suggestion that the king's judges should hold the Assizes within the Liberty. They were therefore held outside, at Street. And – John of Glastonbury could not resist recording – the canons of Wells were put in their place by the Archbishop when they claimed a major role in the blessing of the Holy Chrism. They had no such claim, Kilwardby decided, since their bishop was far away and since the ceremony took place in the abbey church.

So the king paid his own expenses until the last day of his stay and then, on Easter Tuesday, King Arthur's tomb was ceremonially opened. Within were found two separate bones of the king of 'wonderful' size and the delicate and beautiful bones of the queen. Next day the living king and queen wrapped most of the bones in precious palls, marking them with their seals, keeping out only the heads and knee-joints 'for the people's devotion'. The tomb was then closed again, leaving on the inside an inscription recording the event which had been witnessed by the whole of the English Court including the Earl of Lincoln and the Count of Savoy. Abbot John had proved himself a great defender of Glastonbury's liberties and a great promoter of Glastonbury's hero.

Exactly two hundred years later William Wor-

The church of The Holy Trinity, Street

cestre visited Glastonbury. Curiously, he recorded the hollow between the two stone crosses where the bones had been found, but his surviving notes make no mention at all of the tomb. But it was still there: Hugh Forester, the abbey almoner in 1446–7, paid the sacrist the sum of 2 shillings for 'scouring the tomb of Arthur', and his successors paid similar sums until the Dissolution. The last visitor to record the tomb in position was John Leland. In the choir, he noted, were three tombs: King Edward the Elder on the north, King Edmund Ironside on the south, and in the centre 'Arcturus'. 'Here lies Arthur, the flower of kings, the glory of the kingdom', he quoted from the inscription on one side of the tomb, 'whom custom and learning commend by constant praise'. And below, at the foot: 'here lies buried the fortunate wife of Arthur whose virtues merit the promise of heaven'.

Leland's brief notes suggest that at the head of the tomb was carved a crucifix with two lions and some words recording the part Abbot Henry de Sully had played in bringing the bones from the abbey churchyard. At the foot were a figure of Arthur and two more lions. And on the top of the tomb was a cross, presumably the leaden cross which had been found in the grave in the churchyard. Archaeologists examining what they presumed to be the site of the tomb in 1931 found a substantial ashlar base, quite empty.

THE CULT
OF
ST JOSEPH

'For what are men better than sheep or goats that nourish a
blind life within the brain, if, knowing God, they lift not hands
of prayer.' Tennyson: MORTE D'ARTHUR

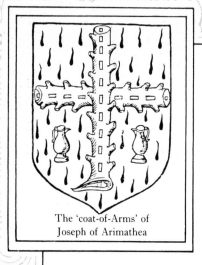
The 'coat-of-Arms' of
Joseph of Arimathea

ABOUT the middle of the 13th century, when King Arthur had been firmly established at Glastonbury, the History written first by William of Malmesbury was given a new and final addition. This was the story of how Joseph of Arimathea, placed at the head of twelve disciples by the Apostle Philip, was sent over to Britain. Here, at the bidding of the Archangel Gabriel, he built the first church at Glastonbury. A note in the margin beside this addition added that Joseph had come with his son Josephes and that he had died at Glastonbury. Readers were referred to a book of 'the deeds of the famous King Arthur', to 'the Quest of Lancelot de Lac' and to 'the Quest of the vessel which there they call the Holy Grail'.

A century later John of Glastonbury told a much more detailed story, beginning with a statement that, according to the 'Book of Melkin', Joseph was buried in a marble tomb at Glastonbury 'on a two forked line next the south corner of an oratory fashioned of wattles', and that in his tomb were placed two silver cruets, filled with the blood and sweat of Our Lord. Then, using a popular book called the 'Gospel of Nicodemus', John recounted some of the earlier activities of Joseph: how, arrested for burying the body of Jesus, he had been miraculously rescued from his prison cell by angels; how he and his son became disciples of the Apostle Philip; how he witnessed the Assumption of the Virgin. And then how, at Philip's request, he had

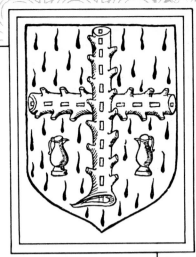

come to Britain and to Glastonbury.

And now John of Glastonbury added a marvellous story from another source, from a book called 'The Holy Grail'. It was a story which told that 600 and more men and women, following Joseph and Josephes, took vows of chastity until they should have come to a land appointed for them. All but 150 broke their vows, but a faithful remnant crossed the sea on the shirt of Josephes on the night of Our Lord's resurrection. When the rest repented they were collected by a ship made by King Solomon and preserved for just that purpose. And so Joseph and Josephes and their disciples finally reached Yniswithrin, the Glassy Isle.

Now at this point John of Glastonbury has to be followed very carefully. He says that the death of Joseph of Arimathea is recorded in the 'book of the deeds of the glorious King Arthur', and in that part of the book which describes a search by the companions of the Round Table for a famous knight called Lancelot de Lac. In the same part of the book, so John records, there is mention of a mysterious fountain which changed taste and colour (so a hermit told Gawain), and a story of the White Knight who explained to Galahad at the beginning of the quest for the Holy Grail the mystery of his miraculous shield.

Joseph of Arimathea was thus firmly established at Glastonbury, but to make quite sure of his 'historical' credibility he was made the ancestor of

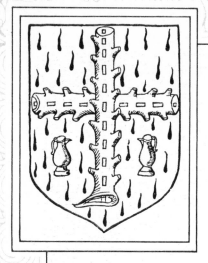

King Arthur himself. So runs the geneaology: Helains, Joseph's nephew, begat Josue, and Josue Aminadab, and from Aminadab in five generations to Ygerna 'of whom King Uther Pendragon begat the noble and famous King Arthur'. And, to make doubly sure, Peter, Joseph's cousin and king of Organia, begat Erlan and so in four generations to Loth, who married Arthur's sister and was the father of Gawain.

Joseph was thus both founder of Glastonbury and ancestor of her most famous son. But no connexion was made between the abbey and the Holy Grail. The Grail itself was a Christian form of the magic healing cup of Celtic legend. It had become the sacred dish of the Last Supper, begged by Joseph from Pilate to catch the drops of Our Lord's blood from the Cross; and hence for some it was the Cup of the Last Supper. The High Romances tell how Joseph brought the Grail with him to Britain; the Grail sought by King Arthur and his knights on their Quest. In the Romances Avalon is occasionally mentioned but – and this is important – Glastonbury never claimed to have anything to do with the Grail. Instead it substituted the tradition of the cruets. That claim gave Glastonbury a direct place not only in the first Christian mission to Britain, but also with the events of the Crucifixion itself.

That was a claim which not even Canterbury could answer. It gave the Abbot of Glastonbury precedence among his brethren in England; and at international

The Holy Thorn and St. Patrick's Chapel, Glastonbury

The east end of the Lady Chapel Undercroft, Glastonbury, once the shrine of St. Joseph of Arimathea

St. Joseph of Arimathea, Langport church

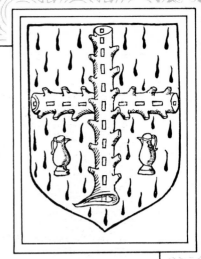

national Councils in the 15th century, when the French claimed seniority on the strength of St Mary Magdalene, Martha and Lazarus, whom they said had preached in Provence, and the Spanish because of their conversion by St James. Glastonbury's tradition of St Joseph gave the English the victory.

At home in Glastonbury by the end of the 14th century there was more physical evidence of the cult of St Joseph. In 1382 Abbot John Chinnock rebuilt a chapel in the cemetery, and in it placed the images of Joseph, Nicodemus and of Our Lord being taken down from the Cross. By about 1500 there was more to be seen. A poem called 'the Lyfe of Joseph of Armathia' written about 1502 and printed (so popular had it become) in 1520, recorded how miraculous cures were being performed in a crypt chapel of St Joseph, apparently under the eastern end of the Lady Chapel, its position still marked by the words JESUS, MARIA on the wall outside. This chapel was, it seems, extended under the whole Lady Chapel as the cult grew in popularity. Thus was unwittingly destroyed the best archaeological evidence of Glastonbury's origins!

William Good, who died an exiled Jesuit in Naples in 1586, remembered serving as an altar boy in St Joseph's chapel about 1535 when he was eight years old. He remembered, too, seeing the chapel destroyed when the abbey was dissolved. By that time, thanks to the devotion of Abbot Richard Bere (abbot 1493–1524) who may well have created the

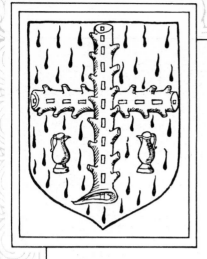

crypt chapel, St Joseph's 'arms' could be seen in several places outside Glastonbury. A green cross raguly with the two cruets and a background of blood drops, can still be seen in painted glass in the chancel of St John's, Glastonbury. A cross and the cruets record Abbot Bere's work inside and outside St Benignus's church, Glastonbury, and at the rear of his house at Sharpham. The same coat of arms is carved on a pew at North Cadbury and the saint himself is pictured in glass in Langport church and in the screen at Plymtree (Devon).

The image of St Joseph and the chapel in which it stood were destroyed with the rest of the abbey in 1539 but the story of the Grail and the Quest was still remembered. In the 18th century the special properties of the water springing from the sandy beds of Middle Lias limestone in the valley below Tor Hill were recognised. A spa was established in Magdalen Street and for a time people flocked to Glastonbury again. Early in the 20th century those same waters took on a new phase in their persistent story.

Malory told at the end of his Le Mort D'Arthur how Lancelot had retired to a valley between the hills near Glastonbury, the valley described but not named in the great Romances of the Grail. Might this not, indeed, be the place where lies the Chalice of the Last Supper? Are not the stones in the well shaft at Chalice Well still stained red?

That well shaft has been studied by archaeo-

The Chalice Well

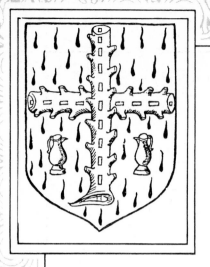

logists, who are generally agreed that its squared lias blocks are similar to pieces used in the abbey in the 12th century. It is therefore possible that the shaft was designed to improve the abbey's water supply after the fire of 1184, and that it was built about 1220. Whether the shaft was a free standing building at that time, forming a well-house, or was more as it stands today has yet to be established.

The well has borne the name Chalcwelle or a variant since at least 1210; and Chilkwell Street, so called at least since 1265, is named after it. The name presumably comes from the limestone source of the water. But the name Chalice Well is so close; and the mystery of the water has had a profound effect on many. For much of the 20th century the well has formed the focal point of a shrine, and its modern lid symbolises the Bleeding Lance and the interlocking Visible and Invisible worlds. So does the magic of the Glastonbury Legend span the centuries.

PILGRIMS

TO

AVALON

'What record, or what relic of my lord should be to after time but empty breath and rumours of a doubt?' Tennyson: MORTE D'ARTHUR

THERE is no doubt that pilgrims came in their thousands to Glastonbury before the Reformation. Ever since the 2nd century saints had been publicly venerated; church dedications from the 7th century and liturgical calendars from the 8th show how cults were established in England, their growth encouraged from the late 7th century by writers of saints' Lives such as the Venerable Bede, who aimed to foster the devotion of the people by stories of miraculous deeds. By the early 11th century a list of about fifty English shrines was compiled, but Glastonbury did not then appear. Another such list survives from the 14th century, and by that time Glastonbury had a prominent place.

William of Malmesbury and Caradoc of Llancarfan in different ways established Glastonbury as a shrine, and the claims of the monks in defence of their abbey had made a collection of relics and records sometimes of doubtful veracity. Royal patronage from Saxon times had brought it an estate which made it the largest landowner in Somerset, arguably the richest monastic house in Britain. Glastonbury's liberties had been established, and the bishops of Bath and Wells were effectively excluded from the Twelve Hides, the heart of the abbey's lands. But, above all, its magnificent buildings occupied the holiest site in the land, holy because it held the bodies of saints whose witness took the history of Christianity back to its very beginnings in Britain and beyond.

According to the fantastic charter of St Patrick, Glastonbury offered to her pilgrims greater privileges of indulgence; ten or even thirty years exemption from purgatory gained by St Phagan and St Deruvian from Pope Eleutherius, twelve years through St Patrick from Pope Celestine, and thirty more, again through Phagan and Deruvian, for those who would actually attempt to climb the Tor.

In 1247 a scribe working among the muniments made a list of Days of Indulgence offered by charters which had been lost but which had been accepted and confirmed by Pope Innocent III between 1198 and 1216. The earliest of the 17 charters, quite probably a forgery, was a grant of 100 days indulgence by St Dunstan. Archbishop Lanfranc gave 30 days, Bishop Reginald 100 (probably at the dedication of the new Lady Chapel after the fire), Bishop Savaric 100 days, Bishop Jocelin 30 days. Forgeries or not, the attraction of a pilgrimage to Glastonbury was apparent.

And when pilgrims came, there was plenty to see: 'the stone pavement, the sides of the altar, and the altar itself are so loaded, above and below, with relics packed together that there is no path through the church, cemetery, or cemetery chapel which is free from the ashes of the blessed', wrote John of Glastonbury. The abbey was, par excellence, the resting place of saints. Here lay St Patrick, St

Anno post passione do-
mini xxxi duodeca sca ex quib;
Joseph ab arimathia primus erat lhuc
uenerut qui ecciam huius regni prima in hoc
loco costruxerut qua xpc in honor sue mris z locu p
coru sepultura psencialit dedicauit sco dauid mene
ueciu archiepo hoc testate Cui dns ecciam illa dedica
re disponieti in sopnis apparuit z eu a proposito reuo
cauit necno i signu qd ipe dns ecciam ipam priu cu
cimiterio dedicarat manu epi digito pforauit z sic p
forata mltis widetib; i crastio apparuit postea uo ide
epc dno reuelate ar scop junio in eade crescete quedi
cancellu i orientali parte huic ecce adiecit z i honore
beate uirginis cosecrauit Cui altar iestimabili
saphiro i perpetua huius rei memoria isigniuit
Et ne locus aut quntitas partis eccie
p tales augmetacoes obli
uioni tradet erigitur

/hc colupna iliniez p
duos orientales agulos
eiusz eccie usq indiem p
tracta zpdictu cacellu ab ea obscin
dente Et erat eius logitudo ab illa linea usq oc
cidente lx pedu latitudo uo eius xxbi pedum
distancia centri istius colupne a pucto me
dio it pductos angulos xlbiij pedum

Brass plate from the cross which once stood on the north side of the Lady
Chapel, Glastonbury

Dunstan, St Gildas and others inextricably bound up with Glastonbury's past. Here, too, were the bodies of saints collected by Saxon kings and nobles and given to the abbey from Ine's time onwards, including Aidan, Paulinus, the Venerable Bede, Benedict Biscop, and the Abbess Hilda of Whitby, all the flowers of northern Christianity. Here were St David (brought by a noble matron) and St Illtud, flowers of Wales. And, lest these possessions might seem a little parochial and narrowly nationalistic, there were representatives of the Church Universal: the disciples of the Apostle Philip, including St Joseph of Arimathea; St Urban, pope and martyr; St Apollinaris, disciple of the Apostle Peter; St Vincent, protomartyr of Spain. And, of course, from a different kind of universality, King Arthur and Queen Guinevere.

Relics could be, as it were, circumstantial as well as personal. There were from Old Testament times parts of the rods of Moses and Aaron, some manna from the wilderness, and a piece of the tomb of Isaiah. And from the New Testament, fragments of the swaddling clothes and the manger from Bethlehem, part of a jug from Cana whose contents had been changed from water to wine, many fragments of Our Lord's clothing and relics of his Passion, including part of the Crown of Thorns and some of the hole which the Cross made on Calvary. There were personal relics of the Virgin, of the Apostles, Martyrs, Confessors and Holy Virgins; the list was

almost endless. So Glastonbury was holy ground, a place chosen by kings and princes: 'the chief personages of the country . . . would rather await the day of resurrection in the monastery of Glastonbury . . . than anywhere else'. So holy, indeed, was the church and cemetery that sinners could not rest there for fear of apparitions; animals and hunting birds were known to drop dead there, and those facing trial by ordeal praying there leapt for joy at their salvation. So well known was Glastonbury abroad, John of Glastonbury claimed in the 14th century, that foreigners sent for samples of its holy earth against the time of their own burials, and could not understand why English pilgrims travelled across the sea to foreign shrines when they had such a holy place at home. Even the Sultan (of which land is not stated) knew something of the place and demanded of an imprisoned pilgrim to the Holy Land a glove filled with the soil of the cemetery where Joseph of Arimathea was buried. 'Those who live there', declared the Sultan, do not know 'what virtue there is in that earth'. The Sacristan of Glastonbury publicised the story 'so that, as the fame of the spot's sanctity grew, those who dwelt there might become holier, while those who lived elsewhere might be more inclined to honour the place in the future'.

Is there just a suspicion of special pleading in these marvellous stories, and is it possible that the abbey was still not achieving its maximum visitor

potential? There had clearly been visitors there, but perhaps not enough. Henry III in 1243 gave the abbey a charter to extend the fair on the Tor from two to five days, and surely some of the buyers and sellers would spend some time in the holy places? The heads and knee joints of Arthur and Guinevere were deliberately kept out of the great tomb in the choir in 1278 for public display. People would surely be interested to see the crystal cross given by the Virgin to Arthur at the Mass at Beckery, which was carried every year in procession on Wednesdays and Fridays in Lent. In the late 1340s even 'the common people' knew the crucifix from which blood had flowed when it was damaged during the attack on the monks in Abbot Thurstan's time.

But if there is some doubt about the success of Glastonbury's publicity in the 14th century, it is clear that by the beginning of the 16th a change had come about. In the 1380s or a little later a visitors' guide was produced. It was made from folding wooden boards and was probably fixed to a pillar in the abbey church. It summarised, remarkably briefly, the story of the monastery as told by John of Glastonbury, mentioning at the end the rebuilding of the cemetery chapel by Abbot Chinnock in 1382. This guide would have formed the starting point of a pilgrim tour, first of the abbey church and its precinct and then of various sites in and around the town where the story of Arthur and Joseph might be brought more fully alive.

Inscription on South Wall of Lady Chapel, Glastonbury

In the choir of the abbey church, to begin with, was the tomb of Arthur and Guinevere, on which lay the leaden cross by which their bones had been recognised, and through which Glastonbury had been identified as Avalon. Next, beneath the Lady Chapel at the western end of the great church, was the crypt chapel of St Joseph, small at first but extended by Abbot Bere about 1500 to cope with the sick who flocked there – from Wells, Doulting, Banwell, Ilchester, Yeovil, Milborne Port, Compton and Pilton for certain, and surely from many other places beyond Somerset as well.

Outside, to the north of the Lady Chapel, a stone cross marked the eastern end of an old chapel which had stood there before the fire. The cross bore a metal plate telling the story of the coming of St Joseph of Arimathea, the dedication of the first church, and the buildings and gifts of St David. On the south side of the Lady Chapel was the abbey's ancient cemetery. The visitor coming through the carved and painted south doorway might first look at the JESUS MARIA inscription on the wall, marking the former entrance to the little crypt chapel of St Joseph. And then, looking across the hallowed plot, the pilgrim could see, as William Worcestre saw in the 1480s, the two ancient cross shafts bearing the names of the ancient abbots, and the hollow between them whence the bones of Arthur and Guinevere had been taken. And 'harde by', as the visitor was told about 1500, grew a new marvel: a walnut tree,

Inscription on South Wall of
Lady Chapel, Glastonbury

protected by a wall, which did not come into leaf each year until St Barnabas's day, 11 June.

From the precinct of the abbey church the pilgrim could go out by the main entrance into High Street. Passing to the top of the town and then along Chilkwell Street, the road skirted the barton of Glastonbury manor, including the great barn, and then the well at the foot of Tor Hill. After that came a sharp climb through the rabbit warren to St Michael's chapel on the summit.

From there the next leg of the circuit could be seen; back past the barton again and then westwards, up the gentler slope of Wearyall Hill, above the abbot's park. There, so the story went, was once a nunnery where Arthur often stayed. And there, for all to see, according to the 16th century author grew 'thre hawthornes also . . . (which) do burge and bare grene leaves at Christmas as freshe as other in May'.

From Wearyall the route led down to the edge of the moors, to Beckery, once the home of St Bridget. Here stood the chapel, or rather its successor, where Arthur had witnessed the Mass of the Virgin and where he was given the crystal cross by the Virgin herself. And after that, perhaps, across the Brue by the Pons Perilous, to yet another part of the Arthur story. When Abbot John of Taunton had stood up for the liberties of his house during the royal visit in 1278 and packed the king's justices out of the Twelve Hides into Street, some of the cases

The George and Pilgrims Inn, Glastonbury

were heard before the king himself. And they were heard in the chapel of St Gildas. Could this be the place where Gildas had retired from the community across the river, as Caradoc of Llancarfan had written? Well, perhaps not exactly; for the church Gildas built was dedicated to the Holy

The ancient Market Cross, Glastonbury

Trinity. But still in 1545 there was a chapel of St Gildas in Street; and still, near the river and curiously isolated from the modern town, stands the parish church of the Holy Trinity.

Back into Glastonbury, passing the newly built meat market and stalls and Abbot Bere's Tribunal, might not the weary pilgrim return to his lodgings? The better-off would surely choose the George Inn, completely rebuilt by Abbot John Selwood about 1473 when the new tenants, David and Edith Adam, paid the large sum of £7 6s 8d for a lease of the 'great hospice'. The annual rent was only 12d, the value of the site and not the business, but somehow by 1500 John Stowell, then the host, was in arrears for that small sum and more besides.

So Glastonbury offered many attractions to its visitors, but what did the abbey receive in return? Its financial records have not survived well, but the accounts of two Receivers mention alms. Brother Alexander Colyns accounted for gifts amounting to £4 5s made in the abbey church in 1503–4, and Brother Thomas Dunstan, Receiver in 1525–6, recorded the sum of £10 9s 9d received as alms in the church and a further £17 4s 10d passed on to him by

91

The Tribunal, Glastonbury

Brother John Milton for alms received elsewhere. Such sums were insignificant in the abbey's great financial machine, but it was not simply a matter of money. The prayers of the faithful, too, still counted for something at Glastonbury in the decades before the Dissolution.

Those years witnessed a remarkable revival in the number of men entering the community, a revival probably inspired by Abbot Richard Bere (1493–1525). Bere himself had come into the community in the 1470s. He was a man of wide sympathies: 'good, honest, virtuous, wise and discrete', said a contemporary, a man fully aware of his additions to their already magnificent church: the chapel of Our Lady of Loretto, whose cult he had encountered in 1504 when he headed an embassy to Pope Pius III in Rome; the chapel of the Holy Sepulchre, where he was later to be buried; and the enlarged crypt of St Joseph under the Lady Chapel. This last addition, together with the work on the magnificent Edgar chapel which he began, showed Bere's awareness of how Glastonbury's glorious past could be exploited.

It was in this same spirit that the old argument with Canterbury over the remains of St Dunstan was revived in 1508. Abbot Bere made a new shrine and placed there the precious relics of his great predecessor. When the monks of Christ Church heard of it they protested to Archbishop Warham and opened their own shrine to make sure the bones were intact. Inside the inner leaden coffin they discovered a

The Bishop's Throne, Glastonbury Pilgrimage

Glastonbury Tor from the top
of Wearyall Hill

tablet with the inscription 'Here lies St Dunstan, archbishop'. Glastonbury monks knew all about inscriptions in coffins and were quite unmoved. Abbot Bere excused himself on the grounds of ill health from visiting Canterbury to inspect the evidence in person and the matter was dropped.

Bere's contribution to revival was apparent in one further way. From 1505 onwards recruits to the community took new names in religion, names of the holy men who had long been revered in the abbey. John Phagan and John Deruvian, Martin Indracht and John Patrick covered the whole span of Glastonbury's history. They adopted the names of Saxon kings whose contributions to Glastonbury's greatness were much less open to doubt. And among them were John and William Joseph, Robert and John Armathy or Abaramathia, Robert Gylde, Robert Yder and John Arthur. Glastonbury in the years before the Dissolution was as aware of its glorious past as it had ever been.

THE TOR

The Tor is a landmark for miles, a constant reminder in medieval times of the far-seeing eye of the Abbot of Glastonbury. And it stands out in the story of King Arthur and Glastonbury for here, according to Caradoc of Llancarfan, was the stronghold of Melwas, King of the Summer Country.

To this lair Melwas brought Guinevere, whom he had abducted from her lawful spouse; and King Arthur came here with an army from Devon and Cornwall to retrieve her. The Abbot of Glastonbury and Gildas brought peace between the warring parties, Guinevere was restored, and the grateful king gave much land to the Church.

Some unknown writer produced a different story, amazing in its boldness and ingenuity. This story is the concoction known as the 'Charter of St Patrick'. It was probably not dreamed up until the early years of the 13th century, but it purported to be written by the saint himself in the 5th. It tells how Patrick, having finished his work in Ireland, came to Glastonbury. Here he found twelve brethren living as hermits (one called Wellias, just to show that Wells was subordinate to Glastonbury even then). These twelve, 'imbued with the rudiments' of the Catholic faith and of 'pious conversation', were the successors of two holy men, saints Phagan and Deruvian. Patrick was soon elected abbot of the community, and was then inducted into the secrets of their foundation, contained in the writings of the two saints. These writings declared that the Old Church had actually been built in honour of the Virgin by disciples of saints Philip and James on orders from the Archangel Gabriel, and that 'the Lord from Heaven' had dedicated the church himself.

And there was more. The 'Charter' goes on to describe how, some time later, taking with him only

Wellias, Patrick climbed up through the dense wood to the summit of the Tor. There they found an ancient oratory, almost in ruin but somehow imbued with so sweet an odour that they thought themselves already in Paradise. On searching the oratory they discovered a book, badly damaged but still partly legible, which included the Acts of the Apostles and the Acts and Deeds of Phagan and Deruvian. At first they could just make out a passage which described how the oratory had been built by the two saints under Divine inspiration and dedicated to St Michael the Archangel. The book also told how Phagan and Deruvian had lived there for nine years.

Patrick and Wellias stayed on the Tor, fasting, for three months; and then, after learning in a vision that his left arm would wither until Patrick told the rest of the brethren the whole story, they returned to Glastonbury. Thereafter two monks, beginning with the Irishmen Arnulf and Ogmar, were to live permanently on the Tor.

A third story of the Tor completes a remarkable trilogy. St Collen, according to a Life written in the 12th century, came to Glastonbury, but he quarrelled with the monks and took himself off, alone, up the 'mountain'. There he was confronted by the King of the Underworld who tempted him with a vision of a castle, musicians, and dishes of dainties. Not, of course, to be tempted, the saint sprinkled the ground with holy water and the vision vanished.

If all these fantasies failed to encourage visitors to mount the steep slope to the chapel on the summit, the 'Charter' offered ample inducement. Patrick himself promised 100 days pardon to all who would cut down the trees which had made his climb so difficult; and the abbey's historians recorded that Phagan and Deruvian had offered 30 years for all visitors.

Now what is the evidence of sober history? Professor Rahtz' excavations there revealed both significant dark-age Mediterranean imports and some fascinating later finds. Most important, as far as medieval visitors were concerned, was the chapel of St Michael. In fact, the remains of two chapels were found, the first of which was evidently destroyed in the earthquake of 11 September 1275. The second chapel, on the same site, was built a few years after that disaster, for fragments of floor tiles of 1290 or later were unearthed, together with stained and painted glass of the 14th century.

It was a simple, one cell building with a west tower, but only the tower now survives. Among the many finds near the chapel were a small bronze badge of the Virgin and Child and a fragment of a Purbeck marble portable altar — proof that there were visitors at the chapel in the Middle Ages, and that Mass was said there, though perhaps not often. And, splendidly, an account of one of the abbey precentors, the monk-official in charge of services, bears all this out. In 1538–9, the last full year of the

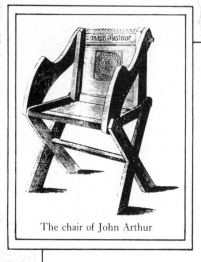
The chair of John Arthur

abbey's life, the precentor paid 16d for candles in the chapel, 1s for repairs, 1s for cleaning, 1s for a chest for the chapel's valuables and 6d for a lock and key (were the visitors stealing the ornaments?). And the precentor paid himself a fee of 6s 8d for saying Mass there on St Michael's day. One final charge was the sum of 1s for cutting nettles there, a rather easier task than felling the trees in St Patrick's time.

Finally, the Tor was the scene of a tragedy, for there on 15 November 1539, the last Abbot of Glastonbury, Richard Whiting, and the two monk-treasurers, John Arthur and Roger Wilfred, were hanged on a charge of robbery for hiding the abbey's plate and ornaments from the King's commissioners. They died, wrote an eye-witness, 'very patiently'. While he lived, John Arthur, bearer of a noble name, had occupied a chair, still to be seen in the Bishop's Palace at Wells. It bears his name and style, John Arthur, monk of Glastonbury.

BECKERY AND POMPARLES: 'The Chapel Right Adventurous and the Dangerous Bridge'

Down below Wearyall Hill beyond the abbot's deer park, where the River Brue flows into the great moor, lies a little island of higher ground called Beckery or Little Ireland. William of Malmesbury recorded the monks' belief that this was a holy place, where the Blessed Bridget of Kildare had stayed for a time, from

The tower arch of St. Michael's Chapel, Glastonbury Tor

St. Mary Magdalene's Chapel, Beckery, excavated in 1967–8. The foundations have now been covered again

the year 488. When she returned home to Ireland she left behind some relics of her stay, namely a bag or wallet, a necklace, a small bell and weaving implements. And, claimed William, they were still preserved at Beckery in the 12th century in her memory.

In the minds of the monks the 'island' had thus been long set apart, but it only came into their possession in a formal way through a charter (probably forged but with truth behind it) granted to them by the Saxon King Cenwalh in the later 7th century.

But what really was at Beckery? Two excavations, one in the 19th century and one in the 20th, have found some answers. First, there was some kind of monastic settlement there in the mid-Saxon period, perhaps after Cenwalh's time. Sixty-three graves were found in association with fragments of wattle and daub, raising the possibility of a timber chapel or tomb shrine, surrounded by a defensive ditch.

Later in the Saxon period, or even after the Conquest, a stone chapel was built there, with other stone and timber buildings nearby. Later still, during the rule of Abbot John of Taunton (1274–91), the island was bought back by the abbot from some powerful tenants-turned-owners, and the chapel was 'lavishly' rebuilt.

Archaeologists agree with the Glastonbury historian, Adam of Domerham, about Abbot John's chapel, but there are still some problems about Beckery. After William of Malmesbury's time a new

The Well Cover, Chalice Well, Glastonbury

From Middlezoy across Sedge-moor; the ruined chapel of St. Michael, on Burrow Mump, stands sentinel in the green moors

The Tower of St. Michael's Chapel, Glastonbury Tor

story began to be told which gave the chapel something more than an odour of ancient sanctity. At some time in the later 12th century it was mentioned first that the oratory of Beckery had been dedicated to St Mary Magdalene; but this dedication had been changed to St Bridget after its then more popular erstwhile resident. And, to add a touch of the miraculous, there arose a belief among the 'common folk' that anyone who passed through an opening on the south side of the chapel would receive forgiveness of sins.

In the 14th century, John of Glastonbury told a new story; or rather he brought an incident from another source, the Persevaus, the High History of the Holy Grail, and planted it in Glastonbury. It was another story of King Arthur.

Arthur, according to John, often used to stay at the nunnery of St Peter at Wearyall. There, one night, an angel appeared, telling him to go to the hermitage of St Mary Magdalene at Beckery, at dawn. He took little notice and the angel appeared on the second night. Again, the king did not go, but ordered his servant to be ready if the vision should come again. During the next night the servant himself went to the chapel and found there a corpse on a bier, surrounded by candles, with two golden candlesticks on an altar. He stole one of the candlesticks but was wounded by someone as he left. Returning to the king, he confessed, showed his wound and died.

The king thus determined to go as he was bidden. He found the chapel doorway guarded by hands

The Tor and the old Pomparles or Pont Perilous bridge

holding swords, but having prayed to be worthy to enter, the swords disappeared. Inside he met an old, bearded man robed in black. As the king watched, the man began to put on priestly robes and was approached by none other than the Virgin herself, bearing her Son in her arms. The Boy took his place on the altar, was consumed and remained as before. In token of this appearance, the Virgin gave to Arthur a crystal cross, which was thereafter preserved in the abbey treasury. The Virgin and Child then disappeared from view. The old man explained to the king that the corpse his servant had seen was that of a brother hermit from Nyland or Andredesey. The king, for his part, made vows of contrition to the Virgin and changed his shield of arms in her honour. Kings from Brutus until his time had borne three red lions on a silver ground, but now he would bear the Virgin's cross in silver on a green ground, with the image of the Virgin and her Son over its right arm.

This was John of Glastonbury's version of the story; and one phrase from his source, the Persevaus, described the chapel and its site. 'The place is right perilous and the chapel right adventurous'. It was a phrase which John did not use, but which the many readers of the Persevaus would have remembered. John, of course, added other touches: Nyland lay at the western edge of the abbey's Twelve Hides, the core of its ancient holding; and the king's new coat of arms was none other than the arms of the abbey itself.

But the perilous place and the adventurous chapel

took visitors on to another scene in the story. There was a tale, known both to the French and the English, about a lad named Gingelain, son of Gawain. In English the tale appeared in the earlier 14th century as a poem called Libeaus Desconus. It told how Gingelain came incognito to King Arthur's court at Glastonbury. The king, dubbing him knight, called him the Fair Unknown, and offered him the next adventure going. A maiden and a dwarf appeared looking for a champion who would rescue a lady captured in an enchanted castle. Gingelain offered himself, but the maiden scorned him and the dwarf declared he would not be worth a farthing for there were three battles to be won, the first 'at the point perilous, be (by) the chapell auntrous'. Arthur, recalling his promise, blessed the youth and the three set off.

> Upon a faire cause,
> Be the chapel auntrous.
> The knight they gonne y-se
> In armes bright of ble (colour)
> Upon the point perilous.

So here, by the chapel adventurous, the chapel at Beckery, is the point perilous, subtly changed in later versions of the poem to 'pont perilous', the perilous bridge, and a causeway. It was, the monks would point out, the bridge and the causeway by which the road from Glastonbury crossed the moor and the

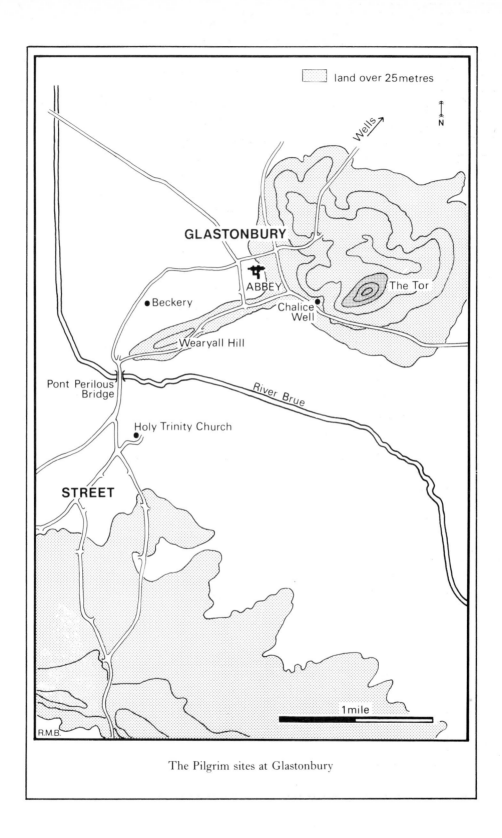

The Pilgrim sites at Glastonbury

The old Pomparles or Pont Perilous Bridge

River Brue into Street.

The bridge was real enough. In Abbot Michael of Amesbury's time (1235–52) it was under the charge of William *pontarius*, William the bridge man. No trace then of another name, simply a bridge. But in 1392–3, John Deor, collector of rents in Glastonbury manor, accounted for income from land 'near Pound perilous'. Another attraction had been created for the visitor. By the time John Leland visited the town in the 1540s its story had changed again. The stone bridge of four arches 'communely caullid Pont perlus' was 'wher men fable that Arture cast in his swerd'. 'Men fable', said Leland: surely local invention again.

The medieval bridge was pulled down in 1826 and its modern counterpart has little romance about it. No longer does the Brue swell to a lake as once it did, at least in winter. And how far is the scene from the bulrush-beds described by Tennyson where Sir Bedivere wheeled Excalibur above his head and closed his eyes and flung him with both hands into the deep!

STRONGHOLDS
OF THE
SUMMER COUNTRY

GLASTONBURY stands in the centre of that land which the Welsh have always called the Land of Summer. It stands overlooking a flat and mysterious basin, once tidal marsh but now an expanse of rich grassland where former islands stand out like stranded whales in a sea of green. Glastonbury Tor, Brent Knoll and Nyland, all later to be part of the abbey estate, or Burrow Mump and Fenny Castle in the hands of lesser lights, each bear significant traces of earlier occupation. And circling round this great green sea are hills to east and south and west, offering superb sites of natural strength, castles in earth and rock commanding wide views across the Summer Country.

BRENT KNOLL: THE MOUNT OF FROGS

A grassy hill 450 feet above sea level, Brent Knoll in ancient winters stood, like the Pillars of Hercules, at the mouth of the Somerset marshes. Before the Romans came the natives had recognised its value: they could see the fortress of Dinas Powis across the Severn Sea, and the Tor across the marshes at Glastonbury. And from there to Cadbury was an easy view. Thus might messages in fire be swiftly sent.

Brent Knoll was obviously, like the other hills, more than a beacon. Its ramparts defended a strong position which still preserves many of its secrets.

Roman debris and burials have been found, and walls were apparently standing in the middle of the 13th century, for Graecia de Meisi, widow of Richard de Cotele, one of Glastonbury Abbey's powerful tenants in Brent Marsh, held a *castellarium*, a little fort, there. And there too, in 1189, another Glastonbury tenant, Richard de Conteville, had land called Batelebergam, still remembered as Battleborough on the lower slopes of Brent Knoll. Was this, as some have said, the site of a battle between Alfred and the Danes, or maybe there is a different origin altogether?

Brent Knoll, its villages of South and East Brent, and the rich marshland around, were themselves pawns in the battle between Glastonbury and the bishops of Bath in the 12th century, and the monks had to marshal all their forces to their defence. That campaign involved the production of title to legal ownership or, perhaps more telling, evidence of long-standing possession.

William of Malmesbury knew that Glastonbury had owned Brent at the time of Domesday in the 11th century. He believed, further, that the land was named after Bregden, an ancient whose name appeared on the taller of the two cross shafts in the monks' graveyard. The abbey later produced a charter, copied into their Great Chartulary or register of title deeds, by which King Ine granted to Abbot Haemgils the land at Brent Knoll in the year 663. The date is obviously wrong, for Ine did not

Brent Knoll, the Mount of Frogs

become king until 688, but there was probably truth behind the forgery; and the careful William of Malmesbury corrected the date to 690.

But that was not sufficient title when the Bishop of Bath was snapping at their heels, so the monks perpetrated another forgery, known as the Great Privilege of King Ine, which the king is said to have given in 725. This document began by declaring Glastonbury's unique origin – 'the church which the great priest and highest bishop with the help of angels had once dedicated with many unheard of miracles to Himself and the perpetual Virgin Mary, as He revealed to the blessed David'. The charter continued by confirming the gifts of Ine and his Saxon predecessors, including Brent.

And then came the impudence of the forgers, for the Privilege went on to put the bishop in his place. Calling on 'the intercession of Almighty God, the perpetual Virgin Mary, the blessed apostles Peter and Paul and all the saints', the king forbade 'any bishop to presume, on any pretext at all, to establish his episcopal seat, or to celebrate solemn mass, or to consecrate altars, or to dedicate churches, or to confer holy orders, or to do anything at all in the church of Glastonbury itself, or in any of the churches subject to it . . . unless he be invited by the abbot or brethren'. And if 'in his swollen pride' he should fail to follow these instructions, his lands at Pilton and Greinton would be taken away. Episcopal power was brought to its knees.

The bishop of Bath remained totally unmoved by such a forgery, and Bishop Reginald's victory over Abbot Robert not only made a nonsense of the Great Privilege, its outcome left Glastonbury without the churches of South Brent and Pilton, the latter lost forever despite its holy and apostolic protection. So a second line of defence was clearly called for.

That line was to demonstrate that the abbey had held Brent long before Ine's time, given to the monks by a greater benefactor, none other than King Arthur. Where the story came from is not certain, but it was added to William of Malmesbury's History in the later years of the 12th century. By the 14th century, John of Glastonbury told a fuller version, incidentally showing it to have been borrowed from Wales.

John recounted that one Christmas at Caerleon, Arthur knighted young Yder, son of King Nuth, and sent him to the mountain of Areynes in North Wales where lived three giants, famed for their evil deeds. The mountain of Areynes in Latin is *mons arenarum*, that is the mount of spiders. The version of the name which crept into William of Malmesbury's work is *mons renarum*, the mount of frogs; and according to that version, the mountain was not in Wales but in Somerset, none other than Brent Knoll. The story might surely be used to Glastonbury's advantage.

The story was, on the face of it, a tragedy. The

brave young Yder, anxious to impress the king, took on the three giants and killed them 'in a marvellous slaughter'. Arthur and his companions, following later, found the young man unconscious, worn out by his exertions. Arthur returned home saddened that he had been the unwitting cause of the lad's death, although two versions of the tale say that Yder survived. What mattered to Glastonbury was not a doubtful death, but the consequence: that Arthur established a community of monks – one version says 24, another 80 – to pray for the young man's soul at Glastonbury, giving gifts and land for their support, including Brent Marsh and Polden. That was an ancestry of possession which could hardly be challenged.

DUNSTER AND CARHAMPTON: DINDRAITHOU AND CARRUM

The Severn Estuary was no barrier to the holy men of Wales. They could see the misty heights of Exmoor in the Autumn and the clear colours of the lower land in Spring. This lower land they called the Land of Summer, for then its floods and marshes gave way to lush green pastures for summer grazing. Over those few miles of treacherous sea the monks of Llantwit, that great Celtic Christian centre of learning, could look across to Watchet – their name for the little river inlet 'under the wood' – and could

Dunster Castle and Grabbist
Hill from the ramparts of Bat's
Castle

St Decuman's Well

pray for courage to face the pagan and unruly people on the other side.

Still today along that coast those holy Welshmen and Welshwomen are remembered: at Watchet itself St Decuman, who came over on a hurdle; at Timberscombe the great Cornish saint Petroc. And so westwards to St Brannoc's monastery at Braunton, and from there down the coast to the Camel Estuary, to St Petroc's monastery and last resting place at Padstow. In between the missions planted by the saintly sons and daughters of the Welsh king Brychan are still recalled: John at Instow, Nectan at Hartland, Morwenna at Morwenstow, Juliot at Tintagel, Endelient at St Endellion, Menfrede at St Minver.

Porlock and Carhampton have not forgotten their founders. Porlock's patron saint is Dyfrig, otherwise Dubricius, the great bishop of South Wales and the Welsh borderlands; the man who, according to Geoffrey of Monmouth, was the Dubricius from the 'City of the Legions' (Caerleon) who, having 'lamented the sad state of his country . . . bestowed the crown of the kingdom' upon Arthur.

Carhampton's saint is Carantoc or Carannog, a holy Welsh prince who, journeying first to Ireland, returned to his cave in Llangrannog, on the coast north-east of Cardigan, and then determined to preach the Gospel in the Land of Summer. Where he actually went was in the hands of the Almighty, so he threw his portable altar into the sea and prepared to follow wherever it led him. The altar came to land at the mouth of the river Guellit in the district of Carrum, a land ruled by Cadwy, son of Geraint, and by Arthur, the joint rulers dwelling in a place called Dindraithou. The saint enquired of Arthur whether any had seen his altar, but Arthur prevaricated. He had a greater problem on his mind, a terrible dragon which was plaguing the countryside. If Carantoc could possibly bring it under control then the missing altar might be discovered.

St Decuman's Well

A dragon was as nothing to the saint. The dragon came to Carantoc 'as a calf running to its mother' and he, wrapping his stole around its bull-like neck, led it into Cadwy's hall at Dindraithou. The people threatened to kill the beast which had so terrified them, but the saint saved its life and ordered it to leave the district.

Carantoc's reward was two-fold. Arthur gave him back his errant altar, very glad to be rid of it; he had tried to use it as a table, but everything put upon it had been thrown off. The other reward was the gift of land at Carrum on which to build a monastery.

Now the life of St Carantoc, according to experts, was probably put together from earlier sources in south-east Wales about 1130, just at the time when Caradoc of Llancarfan was describing how Arthur had come with a host from Devon and Cornwall to Glastonbury to make peace between Melwas and Arthur. Whoever brought Arthur to Dindraithou and Carrum will probably never be known, but it is

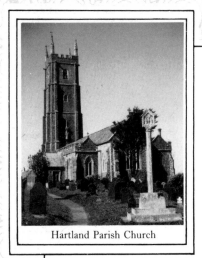

Hartland Parish Church

just possible that Glastonbury's arch-rival, Wells, had something to do with the identification of Carrum with Carhampton. Is it simply coincidence that about 1180, just about the time of Glastonbury's greatest crisis, two churches at Carhampton came into the possession of Wells Cathedral?

One of those churches, dedicated to St Carantoc, was still standing in the early 14th century, but even its site is not now known. The other was the present parish church of St John the Baptist, famous for its fine, late medieval screen. John Leland suggested in the early 16th century – but modern experts would not agree – that the place-name Carhampton is derived from 'Carentokes town'. It is no more accurate in strictly historical terms to suggest that Dindraithou is Dunster, though the Mohun family, owners of the castle in the 12th century, might well have been flattered to think that they were living where Arthur had trod.

Yet there is no doubt that Welsh missionaries came to West Somerset in the 5th and 6th centuries; that the words inscribed on the Caratacus Stone on Winsford Hill recall a land where a Christian chieftain once held sway; that the Christian graves found at Cannington were arranged around the final resting place of a youth in token, perhaps, of servitude, perhaps of fidelity; and that the three hillforts of Bat's Castle, Gallox Hill and Grabbist above Dunster, built in the same tradition as Cadbury and Brent Knoll, may yet reveal that they, a remarkable triumvate, were occupied by a Dark Age warrior chieftain.

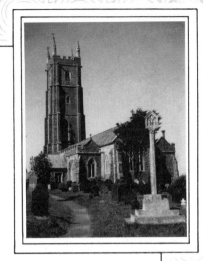

CAMELOT

'a city of shadowy palaces and stately'. Tennyson: IDYLLS OF THE KING, GARETH AND LYNETTE

'Camallate . . . sumtyme a famose town or castelle, upon a very torre or hille, wunderfully enstrength-eid of nature . . .'. So wrote John Leland. Rising massively above the little village of South Cadbury, the hill's wooded crown now masks the ramparts of a great fortress. There was no doubt at South Cadbury in the early 16th century when Leland was there that the site was special. On the top were still to be seen the foundations of buildings, and during ploughing, gold, silver and copper coins of the Roman period with 'many other antique thinges' including a silver horseshoe had been found there.

The names of two nearby villages, West and Queen Camel, also suggested the identification, together with the river Cam that flowed beside them. The name, in fact, is not a satisfactory answer, although Camel may mean bare ridge or rim, certainly a good description of the hills behind South Cadbury today. Yet the name and the archaeology seem to have convinced Leland, or rather convinced the people whom he met there: 'the people can telle nothing ther but that they have hard say that Arture much resorted to Camalat'.

Could this green hill, fortified in times past, be

The ramparts of the Hillfort of South Cadbury. Could this be Camelot?

King Arthur enters Camelot

the centre of the Arthurian world? Camelot of the Legends was a castle surrounded by plains, with a forest and a river not far away; Camelot was the place where the quest for the Holy Grail began; Camelot was the desired resting place of Gawain; and Camelot was destroyed along with all the significant features of Logres when Mark invaded after the death of Lancelot. This is the Camelot of the High Romances, whose site was never named. Somewhere in Southern England, perhaps, until Sir Thomas Malory identified it as Winchester, home of the Round Table, ancient capital of England.

Did Malory's claim give rise to other notions; notions which might have been inspired by political motives? Malory, the Yorkist author, doubtless had Yorkist readers. South Cadbury belonged to the Lancastrian Hungerfords until about 1478 when their sole heiress, a child named Mary, came into the guardianship of the Lord Chamberlain of England. That most loyal of all Yorkists was William, Lord Hastings, Knight of the Garter, well-known retainer of knights. Hastings married the girl to his own son and heir Edward, and it was one of their descendants, the sober Puritan Sir Francis Hastings of North Cadbury, who wrote about 1583 describing Camelot in greater Arthurian detail than Leland even mentioned. Was this part of the Hastings' family tradition, originating perhaps in a piece of Yorkist propaganda, which prompted Sir Francis to describe the 'gallante hil where there hathe bene a

castel in times past called Camelot, wherein Sir Lancelot in King Arthur's time is fayned to have dwelled'? And what of the coat of arms of St Joseph of Arimathea, carved on a bench-end in North Cadbury church? Could that be another piece of Hastings-inspired tradition, linking the place within the popular traditions of Glastonbury?

From the 16th century to the early 20th local traditions have persisted. King Arthur's Palace, the highest point within the ramparts, was spoken of in the 1580s; King Arthur's Well may still be seen beside the footpath which runs below the defences. King Arthur's Hunting Causeway or Arthur's Lane is a notional trackway running northwards from the hill, perhaps towards Glastonbury (crossing the river Alam below Lamyatt Beacon by Arthur's Bridge). It is said that the king still sleeps in a cave within the hill, and once a year a pair of gates swings open for all to see him; and the king and his horsemen ride, either at Midsummer or at Christmas, their horses stopping to drink near Sutton Montis church.

Legend or history, the view across green Somerset to Glastonbury Tor and Brent Knoll is reward enough for the effort of the climb to the ramparts of Camelot. John Steinbeck stood there first on May Day 1959, a golden day, but promised himself he would 'go back over and over . . . at night and in the rain'. But that first day was 'noble gold . . . mystic, wonderful'.

KING ARTHUR
IN
CORNWALL

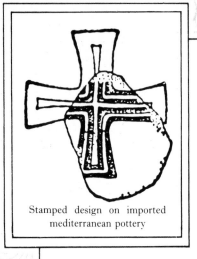

Stamped design on imported mediterranean pottery

THERE are those who claim that the gentle green of the Land of Summer blends imperceptibly into its English neighbours, but there is no doubt that the granite land further west, across the Tamar, is a different world. Advancing Saxons, like the Romans before them, settled comfortably in Somerset and Devon, but found the land beyond less to their liking. The native Celtic people were allowed to keep their ancient ways, their language and their religious enthusiasm, outpost of a world they shared with Wales and Ireland and Brittany. Celtic strongholds still abound in Cornwall, Celtic placenames act as guides to the history of settlement and shrine. Yet of Arthur, the Celtic hero, the traces seem not Celtic, not ancient; rather, they belong to the realm of England, medieval but romantic.

TINTAGEL

'The castle of Tintagel . . . built high above the sea which surrounds it on all sides (with) . . . no other way except that offered by a narrow isthmus of rock'. That was how Geoffrey of Monmouth described the place where Gorlois, duke of Cornwall, sent his wife Ygerna to be safe (so he believed) from the roving eye of King Uther Pendragon. Geoffrey is often, perhaps deliberately, vague about the places he mentions in his history, but there

seems to be no doubt about
Tintagel. It is in Cornwall,
and from the 12th century
that curious headland in the
ancient parish of Bossiney
has borne the name that
Geoffrey used. Geoffrey was
the first, in fact, to use it in
surviving written records,
but that is not to say he
invented it. Indeed, the

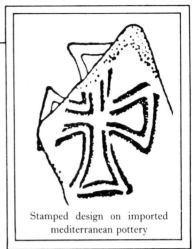

Stamped design on imported
mediterranean pottery

name may be formed in part from the ancient
Cornish word *din* or *dun*, meaning hill or fort. And
so it clearly is, a headland jutting out into the sea,
joined to the mainland by a narrow ridge of rock.

Ygerna, however, was not safe there. While Uther
Pendragon laid siege to Gorlois in Dimilioc, his
passion grew stronger. How could he reach her, for
he was assured that three armed men could defend
the lady at Tintagel against even the strongest army.
Merlin's potions solved the problem. With their aid
Uther was magically changed to assume the form of
Gorlois and was warmly received by a wife over-
whelmed to see her lord come to visit her at the risk
of his life. So there, at Tintagel, Arthur was conceived. Remarkably, neither the deception nor the
death of Gorlois seems to have upset the lady
unduly, and she and Uther 'lived together as equals,
united by their great love for each other'.

Was it simply its romantic situation which led
Geoffrey of Monmouth to place the events at Tintagel? What stood there in his day, or what tales
from the past surrounded it? Perhaps he found the
idea in the ancient stories of Tristan and Isolt; later
versions of the story made Tintagel the site of King

Mark's castle, the place to which Tristan was to bring Isolt as a bride for his uncle and king. There may have been practical reason, too, why Geoffrey used the name, for as he was writing Reginald, Earl of Cornwall, was building for himself a strong castle there. Reginald, an illegitimate son of Henry I, was clearly a man to be flattered by a cleric looking for a patron, as Geoffrey almost certainly was. Was not his whole book dedicated to Reginald's infinitely more powerful half brother Robert, Earl of Gloucester?

Curiously, John Leland, who spent a good deal of time in Cornwall and faithfully recorded Arthurian traditions elsewhere in the country, describes Tintagel castle as he saw it in the 1540s but makes no mention of Arthur. 'A mervelus strong and notable forteres, and almost situ loci inexpugnable', he declared, with a keep on the 'high terrible cragge' surrounded by sea but in his day the feeding ground for sheep and rabbits, approached only by a bridge made of long elm trees.

But if there was no Arthur – and no Mark – in 16th century Tintagel, still there was one thing which suggested a more ancient origin. This was the nearby chapel of St Juliot, one of the children of Brychan, a 5th century king from Wales whose progeny brought the Christian faith to the coasts of Devon and Cornwall. Juliot is, in fact, a somewhat elusive figure, for experts are unsure whether Juliot is male or female, and are divided on the number of

The Tristan Stone, Castle Dore

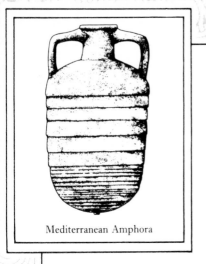

Mediterranean Amphora

probable brothers and sisters – anything between 11 and 62 have been claimed.

Archaeology has revealed something more certain. Excavations on the headland brought to light cell-like structures which have long been identified as part of a Celtic monastic site of the greatest importance, perhaps the Rosnant of ancient Irish tradition. How else could the clusters of primitive stone buildings with earth floors and thatched roofs be interpreted but as the cells of monks? And there was little doubt about the date, for scattered across the site were found fragments of pottery imported from the eastern Mediterranean from the later 5th century onwards. The site, it is agreed, was in use until the 8th century, when there are clear signs of decline.

But there are doubts, for as more and more sites have produced this special pottery, the more they seem to be associated with secular rather than with religious contexts. Was there at Tintagel a chieftain's stronghold before the monastery was founded? Was Geoffrey of Monmouth so wide of the mark after all? When Gorlois fled to Cornwall his army was too small to face King Uther in battle. Instead, he garrisoned his 'castles' and himself took refuge 'in a fortified camp called Dimilioc'. Can this be any place but Domellick, formerly Domeliock, a few miles south-west of Tintagel in the heart of Cornwall, the *din* or fortress of Mailoc in the parish of St Dennis? The farm of Domellick used to include the hill where the church of St Dennis

The rocky crag of Tintagel

Tintagel: the foundations
of the early buildings over-
look a boiling sea

Mediterranean Amphora

stands within the earthworks of an ancient fortress. And not St Denis, patron of France, of course, but *dinas*, a fortress. Mailoc's fortress, not the great stronghold of Gorlois; surely that lies a mile or two north, across Goss Moor, the great Castle-an-Dinas. Geoffrey of Monmouth was clearly no stranger to the traditions and topography of Cornwall.

KELLIWIC

There is another Cornish fortress, a fortress with a longer history than Tintagel, a longer tradition even than Caerleon, the City of the Legions. According to ancient Welsh tradition enshrined in the Triads, the aides memoires of storytellers, there were in the island of Britain in the days of Arthur three tribal thrones. Pen Rhionydd, somewhere in the north, and St David's were two seats of government. The third was Kelliwic, evidently in Cornwall, at once Arthur's home and his capital.

Where was this 'woodland fortress' which the name implies? Callington, Callywith and Barras Nose by Tintagel have had each their supporters, and so have Gweek Wood and Willapark. But the most convincing argument lies with Castle Killibury or Kelly Rounds, a hillfort north-east of Wadebridge, which overlooks the river Camel.

Two other Cornish place names reveal the depth

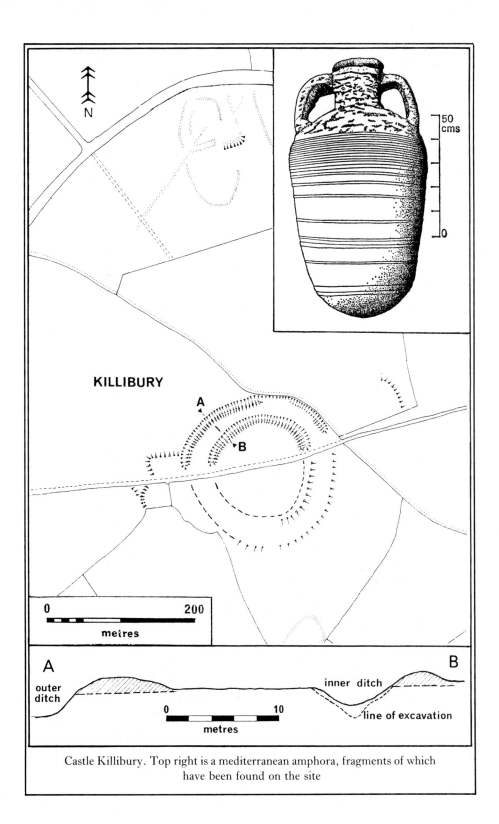

KILLIBURY

0 — 200
metres

50 cms

0

A

outer ditch

inner ditch

line of excavation

B

0 — 10
metres

Castle Killibury. Top right is a mediterranean amphora, fragments of which have been found on the site

of Arthurian tradition. Just by Castle Dore was a farm called Carhurles, 'very possibly', according to Cornwall's historian, Charles Henderson, meaning the fortress (caer) of Gorlois. And may not Tremodret in Roche and Carvedras in Kenwyn be echoes of a homestead and a fortress of Mordred?

CAMLANN

Two vast armies, 60,000 under Mordred, nine divisions under Arthur, faced each other by the river 'Canblam' and there was great slaughter. Mordred the traitor lay dead, Arthur mortally wounded. So said Geoffrey of Monmouth; for him 'Canblam' was without doubt in Cornwall and the Welsh tradition of the final battle they called Camlann was also in south-western Britain.

Leland in the 1540s told how locals near Camelford claimed to have ploughed up bones and harness from a battle where 'Arture fowght his last feld', so the tradition of the site there was very much alive. Yet 16th century archaeology hardly proves a Dark Age battle site, and a later battle in 823 when the Saxon Edgar was conquering the Cornish could be a more likely explanation of the remains. The name Slaughter Bridge, not far from Camelford is, indeed, a most suggestive name, and a site called Arthur's Tomb adds weight for the credulous, but the 'tomb' is actually an ancient funeral slab brought

fatt le chief voler del bu en mi
la place. Ensi q·j· grit mortalite del
roi artu et de mordres son sil la v il
furent tout destruit.

vant li rois artus voit
celui cop si dist trop do
lans. ha. diex por quoi
ne laisies vos tant abaissier de
proesce tiene. Et por lamor de
cestui cop ven ion a dieu mil co
ment icn mozir moi ou mordret
Il tint j· glaive gros z fozt z lais
se corre qusques il puet del cheual
traire vers mordret. Et mor
dret qui bien voit que li rois ne
baiot salui non ocitre nel refuse

The battle of Camlann from a 14th century French manuscript

from some distance in the 18th century which records not the grave of Arthur but the burial place of Latinus, son of Magarus. The worn letters led someone many years ago to see the name 'Atry' there, and perhaps wishful thinking did the rest.

There are more difficulties about Camlann; not with the site so much as with what actually happened. Geoffrey of Monmouth wrote of a great slaughter. Leland told of a single combat on a bridge between Arthur and Mordred in which Mordred first wounded Arthur with a poisoned sword before Arthur struck the fatal blow. Welsh sources, compiled much earlier than Geoffrey, record 'the battle of Camlann where Arthur and Mordred fell' and also make Mordred a hero fighting on Arthur's side. Is this the explanation of the first version of the discovery of the graves at Glastonbury, the version to be found in the records of Margam Abbey, where Mordred shares a grave with his king? Was this version for Welsh eyes only, leaving for West-country consumption the more tragic tale of treachery? Both traditions are, however, essentially agreed: Camlann was the end of an era. The resting, waiting king in Avalon could surely be no more than of spiritual significance.

THE PERSISTENCE

OF

ARTHUR

LEGENDS do not die by political decision or the hangman's rope; rather they flourish. The dissolution of Glastonbury Abbey and the execution of its abbot and two monks in 1539 did not destroy the Legend of Arthur. By the 17th century the three blossoming thorns on Wearyall Hill had become the descendants of Joseph of Arimathea's staff, brought from the Garden of Gethsemane and an offence in the eyes of a Puritan with an axe. That sober Puritan Sir Francis Hastings could write of Lancelot at Camelot without making any compromise to his religious sensibilities. King Arthur was, as he had been from the 12th century, a national, even an international figure. Cornwall may have been the place of his birth and of his final battle, Somerset the base for many of his activities, and Glastonbury his last resting place, but he belonged to the nation.

Several medieval kings had played their part in his 'nationalisation'. Experts now seem agreed that the Round Table at Winchester was made during the reign of Henry III. Edward I's interest in Arthur was clear enough from his visit to Glastonbury in 1278. Edward III's foundation of the Order of the Garter was evidently based on notions of the Round Table; and the extension of the Order by Edward IV reflected the interests of a king who probably knew the author of Le Mort d'Arthur. He was a king, besides, whose illegitimate son by Elizabeth Lucy, nee Wayte, was christened Arthur and bore

Arthur, Overlord of Thirty Kingdoms

many of the characteristics of his handsome, easy-going father. And why Arthur? Perhaps because Elizabeth's home was not far from Winchester, where Malory himself placed Camelot; but perhaps it was simply the king's own wish, another piece of Yorkist propaganda.

Henry VII, looking for 'a worthwhile figure from the British past to include among the pantheon of Tudor ancestors', had his first-born son, born at Winchester, christened Arthur, and placed a statue of the hero-king in the hall of his newly-built palace at Richmond in 1501. Henry's daughter, Margaret, wife of James IV of Scotland, called her second son Arthur in 1509, but buried him within a year. Margaret's son James V, had a son Arthur born and died 1541. Henry VIII, who owed his throne and his first wife to the death of his elder brother, Prince Arthur, had the Round Table at Winchester repainted to impress the Emperor Charles V in 1522. The figure of a Tudor-looking Arthur in the place of honour at the table, and a Tudor rose at its centre, are splendid examples of Tudor propaganda.

Another century but the same throne. Queen Victoria's third son was christened Arthur in 1850. He later became Duke of Connaught and passed his name to his son and his grandson. Arthur was one of the names Prince Albert, later King George VI, was given at his baptism in 1895; one of the names given to his grandson Prince Charles in 1948. The influence of Tennyson is far reaching.

The Round Table, Winchester Castle

And what of more common stock? The choice of a name is sometimes dictated by fashion, sometimes by family tradition. Was it politics or literature, the king or Malory, which influenced Humphrey Nevill of School Aycliffe in Weardale to name his son Arthur in the 1470s or 1480s, and that Arthur to name his son Lancelot? Loyalty to Glastonbury and its traditions obviously inspired John Brooke (d. 1522), the abbey's chief steward, to name his second son Arthur; and other Somerset gentry, like William, Lord Stourton (d. 1548), and Christopher Hadley (d. 1540) named sons after a hero-king. The St Albyns of Alfoxton went further. For several generations down to the end of the 18th century they favoured the name Lancelot, a tradition begun by John St Albyn (d. 1573), who named four sons Lancelot, Tristram, Arthur and George. The name Arthur appeared in the 16th century, too, in the Malet family of West Quantoxhead, the Blakes of Plainsfield, the Bluetts of Kittisford, all in Somerset; and in the Champernouns of Dartington in Devon, but curiously not among the gentry families of Cornwall, although the Trevelyans of St Veep and later of Nettlecombe in Somerset bore as their arms a horse rising from the sea, in recognition of their ancestor who alone swam his horse from St Michael's Mount to the mainland for a wager with other knights of Arthur's court.

Family connexions, and possibly even local politics maintained and spread the name among

Irish landowners from the 16th century onwards, but the source could not have been more English. He was none other than Edward IV's illegitimate son Arthur Wayte. Brought up at his father's court, Arthur was married first to Elizabeth, Baroness Lisle, and second to Honor, nee Grenville, widow of John Basset, the Grenvilles and the Bassets both of solid Devon stock. Arthur, the last Plantagenet, was created Viscount Lisle, served his king at Calais, but came under suspicion of treason. He died, it is said, from relief on hearing he was to be freed from the Tower in 1542.

Lisle's eldest daughter, Frances, married one of his stepsons, John Basset, and their son, Arthur Basset (1541–86) was the ancestor of the Bassets of Umberleigh and the Chichesters of Hall, both in Devon. And he was, very likely, the reason why John Chichester of Hall named his second son Arthur in 1563. That Arthur, 1st Baron Belfast, was the first of the Irish Chichesters, Viscounts Chichester and Earls and Marquesses of Donegall. Arthur Chichester, 1st Earl of Donegall (1606–75), was succeeded by his nephew, another Arthur, son of his brother Colonel John Chichester of Dungannon in County Tyrone. Viscount Dungannon was the title taken in 1662 by Mark Trevor (d. 1670), Governor of Ulster and Marshal of the Irish Army. Presumably he was a neighbour of the Chichesters, probably a friend; and his own family, from Brynkialt in North Wales, had several Arthurs in their pedigree.

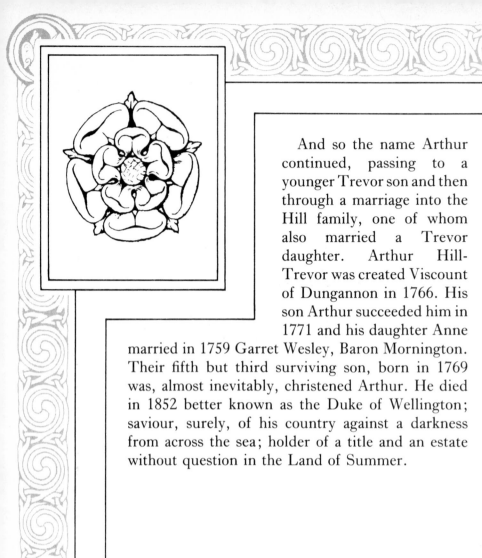

And so the name Arthur continued, passing to a younger Trevor son and then through a marriage into the Hill family, one of whom also married a Trevor daughter. Arthur Hill-Trevor was created Viscount of Dungannon in 1766. His son Arthur succeeded him in 1771 and his daughter Anne married in 1759 Garret Wesley, Baron Mornington. Their fifth but third surviving son, born in 1769 was, almost inevitably, christened Arthur. He died in 1852 better known as the Duke of Wellington; saviour, surely, of his country against a darkness from across the sea; holder of a title and an estate without question in the Land of Summer.

THE ONCE
AND
FUTURE KING

THE concept of a sleeping king who lies ready to save his people at the hour of their greatest danger fulfills the need for certainty in an uncertain world. Arthur is not the only leader who rests until his country needs him, but the confidence he evidently inspired in northern Europe is reflected in claims for his dormant presence in places as far apart as the coast of Norway and the Celtic fringes of France. The heroic, sleeping or not, must never be allowed to die; it is the spirit of the nation.

For a thousand years and more Arthur has entertained and inspired. Each age in need of a hero, each nation in need of an inheritance to be proud of, and several monarchs in need of an ancestry have made of him what they would; have crowned him, clad him in armour, surrounded him with jousts and tourneys. Romances have introduced magic and the sins that flesh is heir to, poets have brought their dreams and artists their visions. The quest for the Grail and deeds of knightly valour have added a purpose and a moral force which have transcended the historic and have confused and obscured a distant reality. For too many people Arthur has become a myth and not a legend.

And the reasons for confusion and obscurity are obvious; the story has been manipulated. Geoffrey of Monmouth, the monks of Glastonbury and the canons of Wells ought not to be seen as the villains of the piece, for we cannot be sure how much they relied upon authentic sources not now surviving. We

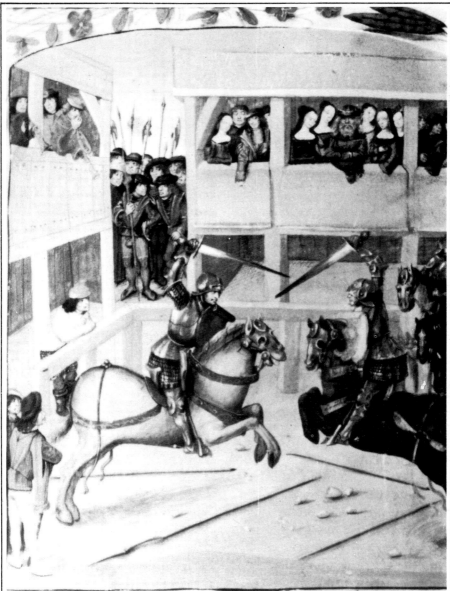

R ceste purtie
nous dist lhis
tour que apces
ce oue la nuit
du tour noient
fu passee et que ce vint a sen
de main matin le roy artue se

fu appareilllie il oy la mes
mier ocurit car il en est
coustumier et pour ce le
ent tous ceulz qui se con
soient a moult preudõm
toist que la messe fu ditte
tous les barons furent all

A tournament before King Arthur

A Vision of Arthur

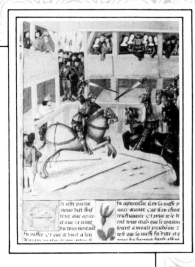

cannot be sure; but we may be justified in our suspicions that their motives had at least something to do with private or community advantage. And yet, in archaeological terms, what are the Dark Ages to the 20th century may well not have been so dark in the 12th. The characters on those cross shafts at Glastonbury were certainly confusing to William of Malmesbury, but they may not have been confusing to some of his contemporaries.

The archaeological element is, indeed, crucial. The sophisticated and organised society so clearly revealed in the refortified hillforts of South-West England must have been led not, to be sure, by a king bearing the attributes of an age not his own, but by one whose success was soon enshrined in the consciousness of his people. Where he was conceived and where he lies was for a later age to decide, for its own good reasons; that he lived and fought to defend his nation is the essence of Arthur.

ACKNOWLEDGEMENTS

Anyone who studies the Arthurian Legends in Somerset owes a great debt of gratitude to Dean Armitage Robinson, whose little book *Two Glastonbury Legends: King Arthur and Joseph of Arimathea* (1926) began the critical study of stories which the monks of Glastonbury had claimed to be history. Professor R.F. Treharne's *The Glastonbury Legends: Joseph of Arimathea, the Holy Grail and King Arthur* (1967) built persuasively upon his arguments, and was my first introduction to the subject. The excavations carried out in recent years by Philip Rahtz at the Tor, Beckery and Chalice Well have subjected those sites to the kind of archaeological scrutiny not undertaken at the abbey itself, but paralleled on many Dark Age sites in the West of England. Geoffrey Ashes's *A Guidebook to Arthurian Britain* (1983) is a fair-minded and balanced commentary on the claims of Arthurian sites throughout the country. Richard Barber's *King Arthur: Hero and Legend* (1986) is his latest splendid work on the literary and historical versions of the Legend. James Carley's edition (now translated) of John of Glastonbury's *The Chronicle of Glastonbury Abbey* (1985) provides in its editorial notes and bibliography a rich vein of secondary, as well as primary, material. His notes have on a number of points inspired my bolder statements and suggestions. W.E. Hampton's vast knowledge of late-medieval England produced the skeleton around which the idea of a Yorkist cult of Arthur emerged. Steve Minnitt read a draft of the archaeological chapter and Richard Bryant has been archaeological adviser, artist and cartographer as well as sympathetic publisher.

I wish to acknowledge the following for the use of illustrations: Mick Aston (colour plate 1); Bodleian Library, Oxford, (colour plate 3, and plates on pp. 2, 41, 153); British Library (pp. 22, 25, 49, 126, 141, 145); Richard Bryant (13, 16–17, 21, 43, 67, 73, 90, 109, 124–5, 139); Professor Barry Cunliffe (18); Jeremy Dunning (119); Jim Hancock (30–31); Hampshire County Council (147); Martin Latham (154); Kevin Redpath (colour plate 4 and pp. 54, 63, 64–5, 74–5, 79, 102–3); Mick Sharp (6–7, 136–7); The Trustees of Glastonbury Abbey (64–5); Jean Williamson (colour plate 6 and p. 101). Other illustrations are by the author.

INDEX

Phagan, John, monk, 96
Pilate, Pontius, 72
Pilton, Som. 53, 88, 115–16
Pius III, pope, 92
Plainsfield, Som. 148
Plymtree, Devon, 78
Porlock, Som. 120
Portchester, Hants. 23
Provence, 77

Quantoxhead, West, Som. 148

Rahtz, Philip, 99
Ralph, archbp. 44
Ramsbury, Wilts. 39
Reginald, bp. 53, 83, 116
Reginald, earl of Cornwall, 36, 132
Richmond Palace, Surrey, 146
Robert, earl of Gloucester, 35–6, 132
Robert, abbot, 52–3, 55, 116
Roche in Tremodret, Cwll. 140
Rome, 12, 19, 92
Roses, Wars of, 3, 8
Rosnant, Cwll. 134; and see Tintagel
Round Table, 2–3, 71, 127, 144, 146–7
Rumps, Cwll. 11

St. Aidan, 85
St. Alban, 15
St. Albyn, Arthur, George, John, Lancelot, Tristram, 148; family, 148
St. Ambrose, 15
St. Apollinaris, 39, 85
St. Benignus, 48
St. Brannoc, 120
St. Bridget, 89, 100, 104–5
St. Cadoc, 33
St. Carantoc, Carannog, 33, 120–2
St. Collen, 98
St. Cyngar, 46
St. David, 57, 85, 88, 115
St. Decuman, 120
St. Denis, 138
St. Deruvian, 83, 97–9
St. Dunstan, 39, 45, 48, 50, 56, 83, 85, 92, 96
St. Dyfrig, Dubricius, 120

St. Endelient, 120
St. Gildas, 19–20, 23, 26, 33, 35, 46, 48, 56–7, 85, 91, 97
St. Hilda, 85
St. Illtud, 46, 85
St. Indracht, 48, 56
St. James, apostle, 77, 97
St. John, 120
St. Juliot, 120, 132, 134
St. Martin, 15
St. Mary Magdalene, 77, 105
St. Menfrede, 120
St. Morwenna, 120
St. Nectan, 120
St. Ninian, 15, 19
St. Oswald, 56
St. Padarn, 33
St. Patrick, 48, 56–7, 83, 97–100
St. Paul, apostle, 115
St. Paulinus, 85
St. Peter, apostle, 85, 115
St. Petroc, 120
St. Phagan, 83, 97–9
St. Philip, apostle, 50, 70, 85, 97
St. Urban, pope, 55, 85
St. Vincent, 39, 85
St. David's, Pembs. 24, 138
St. Dennis, Cwll. 134
St. Endellion, Cwll. 120
St. Gildas de Rhuis, Morbihan, Britanny, 48
St. Michael's Mount, Cwll. 148
St. Minver, Cwll. 120
St. Veep, Cwll. 148
Savoy, count of, 66
Scilly isles, 10
School Aycliffe, Weardale, Durham, 148
Seez, 44
Selwood, John, abbot, 91
Severn, river, 112, 117
Sharpham, Som. 78
Sidmouth, Devon, 14
Slaughter Bridge, Cwll. 140
Solomon, king, 71
Solsbury Hill, Som. 24
Somerset, 4, 8, 10–11, 14–15, 28, 52, 112, 116, 122, 128, 130, 140, 148; and see Summer Country
Stantonbury, Som. 28
Steinbeck, John, 128
Stephen, king, 44

Stourton, Arthur, 148; William, Lord Stourton, 148
Stowell, John, 91
Street, Som. 66–7, 89, 91, 110
Sulis Minerva, 10
Sully, Henry de, abbot, 53, 56, 58, 68
Summer Country, Land of Summer, 13, 27–8, 33, 48, 96, 112, 117, 120, 130, 150; and see Somerset
Sutton Montis, Som. 128

Tamar, river, 11, 38, 130
Tamaris, 11
Taunton, John of, abbot, 62, 66, 89, 104
Taunton, Som. priory, 52
Tennyson, Alfred, Lord Tennyson, 110, 146
Thurstan, abbot, 40, 42, 45, 87
Timberscombe, Som. 120
Tintagel, Rosnant, Cwll. 4, 8, 27, 36, 120, 130–1, 134–8
Torridge, Devon, river, 38
Trethurgy, Cwll. 14
Trevelyan family, 148
Trevor, Arthur, 150; Mark, Viscount Dungannon, 149
Trevor, Hill-, Anne, 150; Arthur, Viscount Dungannon, 150; Arthur, 150
Tristan, Drustan, 27, 131–3; stone, 133

Uffculme, Devon, 44
Umberleigh, Devon, 149
Uplyme, Devon, 38
Uther Pendragon, king, 72, 130–1, 134

Vespasian, 11
Victoria, queen, 146
Victricius, bp. 15

Wadebridge, Cwll. 138
Waleran, count of Mellent, 35
Wales, Gerald of, 58–9, 62
Wales, 4, 14, 19–20, 26–7, 57, 85, 116–17, 120–1, 132; Annals of, 24–5, 32; Triads, 32, 138
Walter, archd. 34
Wansdyke, 28, 30–1
Warham, William, archbp. 92
Watchet, Som. 117, 120
Wayte, Arthur, Viscount Lisle, 144, 146, 149; Elizabeth, 144, 146
Wellias, 97–8
Wells, Som. cathedral, 8, 33, 43, 46, 53, 66, 88, 97, 122, 152; archd. of 53; bp. of, 40, 66; Palace, 100
Wesley, Wellesley, Arthur, duke of Wellington, 150; Garret, Baron Mornington, 150
Westminster abbey, 56
Whitby, Yorks. 85
Whithorn, Galloway, 15
Whiting, Richard, abbot, 100
Wilfred, Roger, monk, 100
Willapark, Cwll. 138
William I, 38–9
William, pontarius, bridgeman, 110
Winchester, 3, 44, 52, 127, 144, 146
Windsor, Berks, St. George's chapel, 3
Winsford, Som. 28–9, 122
Witham, Som. priory, 52
Worcester, bp. of, 53
Worcestre, William, 66, 68, 88

Yatton, Som. 12
Yder, 116–17
Yder, Robert, monk, 96
Yeovil, Som. 88
Ygerna, 72, 130–1
Yniswithrin, Glassy Isle, 62, 71